# COLOR FOR THE LANDSCAPE

## Flowering Plants for Subtropical Climates

Mildred E. Mathias, Editor
Professor of Botany, Emeritus
University of California, Los Angeles

Photography by Ralph D. Cornell, FASLA

Published by
Los Angeles Beautiful, Inc.
California Arboretum Foundation, Inc.
Southern California Horticultural Institute, Inc.
Theodore Payne Foundation for Wild Flowers and Native Plants, Inc.

under the direction of
Dr. Samuel Ayres, Jr., Chairman of Flowering Booklet Committee
Betty Thomas Carriel, print and editorial coordinator

# PREFACE

This book is a complete revision, including many additional species and new color photos, of six booklets previously published by the sponsors. For a number of years the sponsors have been encouraging more color in the landscape through the use of introduced and native flowering plants. In 1964 three of the sponsors, Los Angeles Beautiful, California Arboretum Foundation, and the Southern California Horticultural Institute, published the first booklet on flowering trees and this was followed by booklets on flowering shrubs, vines, and ground covers. In 1967 Los Angeles Beautiful produced a booklet on *Erythrina*, the official tree of the City of Los Angeles. The Theodore Payne Foundation for Wild Flowers and Native Plants joined the other sponsors in 1971 to publish a booklet on Colorful California Native Plants.

SECOND PRINTING 1976

The publishers acknowledge two new sponsors:
Descanso Gardens Guild, Inc., and
South Coast Botanic Garden Foundation, Inc.,
and the activities of Virginia M. Baldwin in coordinating the
sponsorship and distribution of this second printing.

Library of Congress Catalog Card Number: 73-90024
Brooke House Publishers, Inc.
ISBN: 0-912588-14-4



Lithographed in U.S.A. by
GEORGE RICE & SONS

# ACKNOWLEDGEMENTS

The publishers gratefully acknowledge the contributions of the following individuals who assisted in the preparation of this publication:

Dr. Robert E. Atkinson, author, botanical consultant

Fred C. Boutin, botanist, Huntington Botanical Gardens, San Marino

Philip E. Chandler, instructor in ornamental horticulture and senior associate, Chandler & Lang, Landscape Planning, Inc.

Francis Ching, director, Los Angeles County Department of Arboreta and Botanic Gardens

Mrs. Ralph D. Cornell

Henry Davis, publisher of Flowering Booklet series

Merritt S. Dunlap, president, Theodore Payne Foundation, Inc.

Morgan Evans, A.I.L.A.

Myron Kimnach, curator, Huntington Botanical Gardens, San Marino

Dr. Lee W. Lenz, director, Rancho Santa Ana Botanic Garden, Claremont

Elisabeth Marshall, vice-president, Southern California Horticultural Institute, Inc.

Dr. Elizabeth McClintock, curator, California Academy of Sciences

Dr. Katherine K. Muller, director, Santa Barbara Botanic Garden

Gerry V. Patten, line drawings illustrator

James C. Perry, president, Perry's Plants, Inc.

Edward L. Peterson, director, Theodore Payne Foundation, Inc.

James H. Seaman, president emeritus, Theodore Payne Foundation, Inc.

George H. Spalding, botanical information consultant, Los Angeles County Department of Arboreta & Botanic Gardens

Dr. William S. Stewart, director of research, Pacific Tropical Botanical Gardens, Hawaii

Dr. Vernon T. Stoutemyer, chairman emeritus, Department of Agricultural Sciences, University of California, Los Angeles

David S. Verity, botanist, University of California, Los Angeles

Donald P. Woolley, former superintendent, South Coast Botanic Garden

Ralph Dalton Cornell, F.A.S.L.A., 1890-1972

To the memory of *Ralph Dalton Cornell*, dean of landscape architects, inspired plantsman and photographer—whose creative talent, intellect and good taste brought beauty and dignity to everything he touched—this book is dedicated with gratitude.

TABLE OF CONTENTS

Front cover picture: Erythrina caffra, see page 52

# CHOOSING COLORFUL PLANTS FOR YOUR LANDSCAPE

Gardening in subtropical regions is a continuing challenge with a wealth of plant materials, both flowering and non-flowering, available for cultivation. Some of the most beautiful flowering plants from the far corners of the world thrive in subtropical gardens providing a flower display possible only under glass in cooler climates.

The purpose of this book is to present some of the more outstanding colorful plants from around the world, such as *Jacaranda* from South America; many species of *Erythrina* or coral trees of the tropics and subtropics; *Acacia* and flowering *Eucalyptus* from Australia; *Protea* and *Leucospermum* from South Africa; and native California plants such as *Ceanothus, Fremontodendron,* and *Iris*. It is an exciting list of possibilities for enhancing the landscape with the beauty found only in the natural color of flowers.

The book is illustrated with color photographs by the late Ralph D. Cornell of flowering plants successfully grown in southern California and equally useful in other Mediterranean climates having hot dry summers and cool wet winters. Each plant illustrated is identified by botanical name, common name, plant family and area of origin. The minimum temperature that will result in plant damage is given as well as the usual season of bloom or, in the case of plants with colorful fruit, the season of maximum color. The descriptions include size and shape, whether evergreen or deciduous, flower color, microclimate to which best adapted, and special cultural requirements. Where plants are tender or marginal for the subtropics, or so difficult that they are recommended only for the adventurous or advanced gardener, that is indicated also.

Not every plant will grow well and bloom in every garden. Variations in soils and microclimates must be considered in choosing a specific plant for a site. Some plants will flower only in areas with continued heat while others require the moderate cooler coastal climates. Some are best planted against a wall to provide reflected heat. Some need winter chilling to produce flower buds; others need to be kept dry for a dormant period. Most plants do best with good drainage. If your garden has special problems it is best to consult a landscape architect, designer, or your local nurseryman.

For convenience plants are grouped in chapters by plant form or use—as trees, shrubs, vines and ground covers. However plants may fit in more than one category. Some trees make fine shrubs; many shrubs with proper pruning make small trees. Some genera because of their variety of form have been placed in sub-chapters between trees and shrubs. Some shrubs are sprawlers and make excellent vine substitutes while others are best suited for ground covers. Since California native plants often require special garden treatment they are discussed together regardless of form. The reader will find it worthwhile to explore the entire book including the lists of additional plants of merit at the end of each chapter. The plants in this book offer new color excitement and perhaps other advantages in longevity and lower maintenance because of their affinity for the subtropics.

Many of the plants best known because they are grown widely in several climatic zones, such as roses and popular annuals and perennials, have been omitted to provide space for discussion of those especially well adapted to subtropical regions. Many species of the various genera such as *Eucalyptus, Acacia, Escallonia, Arctostaphylos, Buddleia,* and others, also have been omitted. For descriptions of these and for more cultural details, cold tolerances, and other horticultural information Sunset Western Garden Book is a good reference.

# LEARN THE PROPER NAMES

An important factor in getting the specific plant desired for your landscaping objective is to *LEARN THE PROPER NAME.*

If the landscape design calls for a thirty-foot acacia to provide a giant bouquet of yellow flowers in late winter you must specify *Acacia baileyana*. If you ask your nurseryman only for an acacia you may get the equally beautiful *Acacia glandulicarpa,* a spring-blooming compact shrub, or any one of the other acacias in the nursery. More disappointing would be to find out at long last that the mimosa tree you bought thinking it to be the yellow-flowered acacia known as mimosa in the part of the country you came from was the pink-flowered *Albizia julibrissin,* called mimosa in the part of the country your nurseryman came from.

Knowing the botanical name can prevent such mistakes and disappointments. Botanical names are an international language and refer to the same plant wherever they are used while common names vary from one part of the world to another. The use of mimosa and acacia is a good example. The wild lilac of California is *Ceanothus* and not the common lilac of gardens, *Syringa*,in a very different plant family. Jasmine is a common name for the genus *Jasminum* in the olive family but star jasmine is a common name for *Trachelospermum jasminoides* in the dogbane family.

Botanical names are not difficult. They normally consist of two parts, the first is the genus and the second the species name. For example, *Acacia* is the genus name and *baileyana* and *glandulicarpa* are names for two different species of *Acacia* illustrated in this book. Both names must be used and the plants are referred to as *Acacia baileyana* and *Acacia glandulicarpa*. In text where the meaning is obvious the genus name may be abbreviated and the botanical name may be written *A. baileyana* or *A. glandulicarpa*. On occasions the name consists of three parts as in *Eucalyptus leucoxylon macrocarpa* or *Camellia sasanqua* 'Yuletide.' In the case of the *Eucalyptus* the species name is *leucoxylon* and *macrocarpa* is a botanical variety of that species. In the case of the *Camellia* the third name 'Yuletide' is that of a cultivated variety, a cultivar. Botanical names are italicized in the text while cultivar names are not italicized but are capitalized and set in single quotation marks. In a name such as *Clematis* X *lawsoniana*, the X indicates that the plant is of hybrid origin. Some cultivars are selections from hybrids that have not been named so that no species name is used as, for example, *Dimorphotheca* 'Buttersweet.' Many a genus name may have become familiar through its use as a common name such as hibiscus, fuchsia, acacia and eucalyptus. When it is used as a common name it is not capitalized and not italicized.

In the classification of plants similar genera are grouped into a family. Since plant families are often easily recognized by the gardener, even though he may not know the genus, the family name has been included with the descriptions. For example the genera *Acacia, Calliandra, Bauhinia, Cassia* and many others in this book are members of the Leguminosae, a large family of plants that also includes such common garden vegetables as peas and beans. The entire family is characterized by its fruit which generally resembles a bean or pea pod.

Most nurseries will have the plants labelled with both the botanical name and local common names.* Knowing the correct botanical name will make it possible for you to get the plant you want.

*Popular or common names of plants used throughout this book denote those most commonly heard in southern California. It must be reemphasized that common names can be misleading. For example the tree called "coral tree" in California is known as "flame tree" in some countries. And there are completely unrelated trees with red flowers also known as "flame tree." Sometimes the common name refers to many species in a genus and it is essential to know the scientific name to obtain the desired plant.

## SOURCES OF PLANTS

Not all of the plants described or listed in this book are available at all local nurseries. Many commercial nurseries must of necessity stock those plants that are well known and provide income from rapid sales. However most nurserymen upon request are willing to obtain the more unusual plants from wholesalers. Again it is essential that the plant is ordered under the correct botanical name.

The Los Angeles State and County Arboretum is continually introducing many new flowering plants by making stock available to nurseries. The Theodore Payne Foundation is a source for California wild flowers and native plants.

The Southern California Horticultural Institute is endeavoring to bring back into cultivation garden-worthy plants that have gone out of the trade by offering them for sale at each monthly meeting on its Scholarship Plant Table. Along with the arboreta and botanical gardens mentioned they are promoting the introduction and testing of promising new plants for our gardens.

## WHERE TO SEE MATURE SPECIMENS

Mature specimens of most of the plants in this book may be seen in the Los Angeles State and County Arboretum in Arcadia and its branches, Descanso Gardens in La Cañada and the South Coast Botanic Garden on the Palos Verdes Peninsula; the Huntington Botanical Gardens in San Marino; or at the Botanical Gardens and Campus of the University of California in Los Angeles. California native plants may be seen at Rancho Santa Ana Botanic Garden in Claremont, the Santa Barbara Botanic Garden, and at the Theodore Payne Foundation, Sun Valley. These names are often abbreviated in the text to Arboretum, Descanso, Huntington Gardens, UCLA, etc. All other locations mentioned in the text are also in southern California.

## *Chapter I*
# FLOWERING TREES

For Year-Round Color in Subtropical Climates

*Erythrina caffra*
see page 52

Flowering trees in a riot of color are typical of the tropical regions of the world. They adorn not only the native forests but city streets and home gardens. Many do not realize that, with proper selection from a wealth of flowering trees from areas with subtropical or Mediterranean climates, they can achieve a similar kaleidoscope of color as a canopy for the garden. Instead of planting trees that offer no color except the greens of their leaves we can select from the material illustrated in the following chapter, the delicate pink of *Albizia julibrissin*, the golden cassias, the blazing red and orange *Erythrina*, lavender-blue *Jacaranda*, and many others. Trees are the basic, long-lived plants around which we design the rest of the landscape. We must remember that they are not only the providers of shade but that they can be used to enhance the garden with their flowers and fruits. During their flowering season we are rewarded with a colorful display that adds distinction to the garden and excitement to the landscape.

Flowering trees that delight the tourist in Hawaii or the Caribbean area, such as the golden shower tree, *Cassia fistula,* royal poinciana, *Delonix regia,* or African tulip tree, *Spathodea campanulata,* do not thrive in southern California because they are not adapted to a Mediterranean climate with cool winter rains. But all the beautiful color of these plants can be duplicated in southern California with flowering trees from countries with a similar climate, such as Australia, South Africa, parts of South America, and some regions of Asia.

This chapter includes some of the more spectacular flowering trees now being successfully grown in southern California. Only trees known to thrive in Mediterranean climates are presented although some may be best adapted to coastal zones and others to the interior valleys.

The sponsors of this book have been encouraging the use of flowering trees in southern California for many years and the results are now visible in such noteworthy plantings as *Erythrina caffra* along San Vicente Boulevard from Brentwood to the ocean in Santa Monica, *Jacaranda* in many commercial sites, and *Chorisia speciosa* in the Civic Center in downtown Los Angeles. Each home gardener can assist in making California truly colorful by planting one or more of the flowering trees. They will add beauty to the landscape for years to come.

## HOW TO GROW FLOWERING TREES AND SHRUBS

Flowering trees and shrubs are no more difficult to grow than non-flowering ones, and their bouquets offer double dividends. Flowering trees, in addition to their jewel-like beauty, may make beautiful shade and street trees. Some trees, such as the jacaranda, spread carpets of color on the ground with their fallen petals. The small chore of removing them is a little price for their beauty. Proper placement will eliminate even this problem.

1. Select the best species for the site, never plant a tender plant in cold areas, sun-loving plants in shade, or vice versa.

2. Assure good drainage.

3. Dig a hole considerably larger than the container. For a five gallon size plant, mix in one cup of bone-meal in the bottom of the hole. Partly fill the hole with top soil or a mixture of sandy soil and well-rotted compost, never manure.

4. Tamp firmly so ground will not settle after planting.

5. Soak the plant, allow to drain, then remove from can and plant at the same level as the surrounding ground. Fill the balance of the hole with soil mixture, firm down again, and water thoroughly.

6. Keep a basin around the plant at a distance from the trunk. *Never* slope the basin so that the base of the plant is lower than the surrounding ground. To do so invites oak root fungus and other trouble. See diagram.

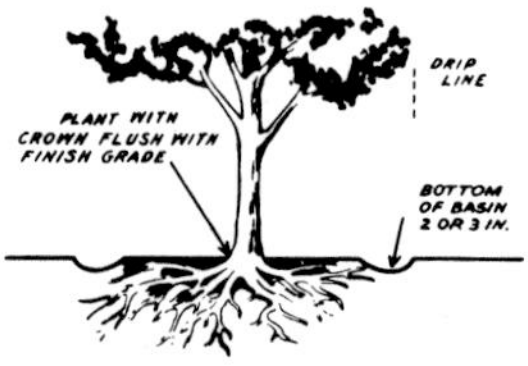

7. Deep-water by slow soaking of ground every week or two, depending on weather, size of plant and soil. Few deeper soakings are much better than frequent shallow waterings. A wilted plant may be revived, but a rotted root is dead!

8. Fertilize only as needed. Many plants from Australia and South Africa resent over-fertilizing. Original bone-meal usually suffices for first year or longer.

9. Prune for shaping and to remove dead wood. Flowering plants should be pruned after flowering unless fruit is also showy, never just before their blooming season.

| ALBIZIA JULIBRISSIN | *Leguminosae* | 10°F. |
| --- | --- | --- |
| Persian silk tree | Summer | Southern Asia |

The rapidly growing popularity of *Albizia julibrissin* has made its soft pink puffs of bloom set off by apple-green fern-like foliage, one of the signs of summer. The tree grows slowly to 40 feet. Its somewhat flat-topped shape with spreading branches provides an inviting canopy of shade in summer and its deciduous nature permits maximum sun during winter. Either inland or near the coast its cultural requirements are minimal, needing only a sunny location. The tropical appearance of this beautiful tree, its graceful form, and the delicate pink glow of the blossoms, make it a worthwhile addition to the southern California landscape.

| BAUHINIA BLAKEANA | *Leguminosae* | 25°F. |
|---|---|---|
| Hong Kong orchid tree | Fall or Winter | Southeast Asia |

This tree produces strong color and distinction for autumn and early winter. The rather large, kidney-shaped, gray-green leaves shed partially to display swelling blossom buds, produced precociously even on small, young plants. The flowers, of butterfly-orchid shape, range in color from cranberry-maroon through rose-purple to orchid-pink, often in the same blossom. They are generally larger than those of the commoner spring and summer flowering species of orchid trees. As is true of most bauhinias, this species seems to be well adapted to southern California areas. Fine specimens may be seen in flower much of the year on the south side of Bunche Hall, UCLA.

| BAUHINIA VARIEGATA | *Leguminosae* | 25°F. |
|---|---|---|
| Orchid tree | Spring | India, China |

This orchid tree is the commonest cultivated in southern California. A 20 to 25 foot subject, it is inclined to bushiness or multiple trunks. It also is extremely variable in its blooming period, foliage quality, and leaf-holding characteristics according to soil, exposure, and weather vagaries. Generally, however, it drops its broadly-lobed leaves in midwinter and produces its principal show of orchid-lavender to purple, white, or even pink, broad-petalled flowers in April, with or without new foliage. Following mild, dry winters, the display is sensational, and blossoms may continue to form intermittently on different sections of the tree, occasionally even into autumn. The plant likes heat but withstands considerable cold. It probably does best on well-drained southeast slopes away from continual ocean wind. Fine specimens occur throughout Los Angeles and at Palm Springs.

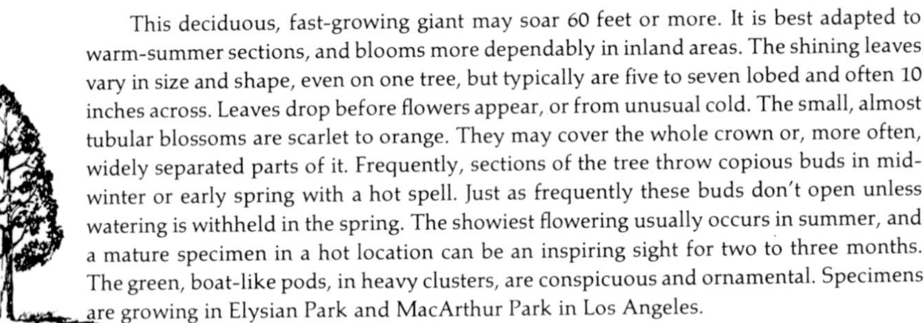

BRACHYCHITON ACERIFOLIUM — *Sterculiaceae* — 25°F.

Australian flame tree — Spring-Fall — Australia

This deciduous, fast-growing giant may soar 60 feet or more. It is best adapted to warm-summer sections, and blooms more dependably in inland areas. The shining leaves vary in size and shape, even on one tree, but typically are five to seven lobed and often 10 inches across. Leaves drop before flowers appear, or from unusual cold. The small, almost tubular blossoms are scarlet to orange. They may cover the whole crown or, more often, widely separated parts of it. Frequently, sections of the tree throw copious buds in mid-winter or early spring with a hot spell. Just as frequently these buds don't open unless watering is withheld in the spring. The showiest flowering usually occurs in summer, and a mature specimen in a hot location can be an inspiring sight for two to three months. The green, boat-like pods, in heavy clusters, are conspicuous and ornamental. Specimens are growing in Elysian Park and MacArthur Park in Los Angeles.

| BRACHYCHITON DISCOLOR | *Sterculiaceae* | 25°F. |
|---|---|---|
| Pink flame tree | Summer | Australia |

Another fine tree for warm inland areas, the pink flame tree (or pink bottle tree) is tall (40 to 90 feet), high-headed, and slightly bottle-trunked. Usually narrowly pyramidal in youth, it becomes more widely spreading in maturity. The six inch somewhat maple-like leaves are woolly white beneath and dark green above. They fall just before the flowers appear. Following sudden cold weather, the entire tree may be bare for a period. Blossoms of rose to pink are backed by short brown wool, which also distinguishes the six inch rusty seed pods. This tree is especially handsome for avenue planting where there is ample accumulated sun heat. Single or grouped specimens may also serve as a focal point or an interesting mass. The pink flame tree usually has few flowers and poor foliage in coastal sections swept by chill afternoon breezes and fog. Splendid, well-grown examples can be seen in the Huntington Botanical Gardens in San Marino.

# THE AUSTRALIAN BOTTLE BRUSHES

*Callistemon, Calothamnus, Kunzea,* and *Melaleuca* are all known as bottle brushes. All are members of the Myrtaceae and there are over 100 species in the four genera. Because of their bright color, long blooming period, hardy nature and the lasting quality of the blossoms in floral arrangements, they are now widely used throughout most regions of the southwestern United States. Most are shrub forms though the two illustrated opposite are small trees. Melaleucas are discussed on page 26. *Metrosideros,* the New Zealand Christmas tree somewhat like the bottle brushes, is illustrated on page 27.

CALLISTEMON CITRINUS *(C. lanceolatus)* *Myrtaceae* 24°F.
Bottle brush Winter & Other Seasons Australia

Of the many bottle brushes grown in California, *C. citrinus,* upper illustration opposite, is most nearly everblooming, and has crimson red flowers. Long treated as a large shrub, this evergreen species is now commonly grown as a small tree. It can be trained into a 20 foot tree with a narrow head and a single trunk. The new leaves are pinkish-copper in color becoming vividly green. Usually it blooms conspicuously in mid-winter, then intermittently throughout the year. Easily adapted to most adversities of soil, wind and water, it is also amazingly tolerant of both heat and cold.

*Callistemon viminalis,* the weeping bottle brush, opposite lower, is a 20 to 30 foot evergreen tree with low-sweeping pendent branches softly clothed in narrow, light-green leaves. The flowers hang in dense spikes of pure red, soft and brush-like, encircling the ends of slender branches in brilliant profusion intermittently throughout the year. The tree may break into full display at any season, especially following periods of high temperatures. Afterwards it rests for six weeks or so, preparing new growth for another show. The fruits hang on for several seasons, covering the mature branches like carved wooden buttons. The weeping bottle brush adapts easily to most reasonably drained California soils. Some heading back and severe thinning of surplus branches to prevent top-heavy growth are desirable. Careful staking and ample water are essential for young plants. Like all *Callistemon* species, iron soil additives may be needed if leaves show yellowing.

*Callistemon lilacinus* is another shrub or tree which grows to as tall as 20 feet and has purple-red blossoms. *C. salignus,* also a small tree, has white flowers and its new foliage is coppery-colored.

Other desirable bottle brushes are *Calothamnus quadrifidus* and *C. villosus,* commonly called net bush. These are six foot needle-leafed shrubs with bright red blossoms formed like tufted ends of a bottle brush.

Kunzeas are evergreen shrubs or small trees varying from prostrate species to 20 feet. Their small brush-like flower clusters are white, yellow, pink or red.

*Callistemon citrinus*

*C. viminalis*

CALODENDRUM CAPENSE | *Rutaceae* | 25°F.
Cape chestnut | Summer through Fall | South and East Africa

The Cape chestnut (unrelated to the true chestnut or horse-chestnut) is grown for its profusion of white, rose and lilac flowers, with brownish purple spots, which are displayed in large clusters from May into July. Mature specimens slowly achieve 25 to 40 feet with similar spread. Leaves are medium green and up to five inches long. The tree is partially evergreen or briefly deciduous, depending upon location and season.

This tree seldom blooms when young, performing best in rapidly-draining soil, deeply and infrequently watered. It reaches its climax in areas not far from the tempering ocean. Viewed in early summer, the two parkway trees on Ohio Avenue, just east of Federal in West Los Angeles, will be a long-remembered horticultural experience. A very large and old specimen may be seen near the old picnic grounds in Elysian Park. Others are in Exposition Park and MacArthur Park, and on the UCLA campus.

| CASTANOSPERMUM AUSTRALE | *Leguminosae* | 25°F. |
|---|---|---|
| Moreton Bay chestnut | Summer or Fall | Australia |

This shining emerald evergreen is round-headed to almost flat-topped. Seldom more than 25 to 30 feet tall and across in southern California, it would be an arresting foliage tree even if it never bloomed. Its large leaves are composed of 11 to 15 leathery leaflets up to six inches long, and remain attractive throughout the year. Slow-growing, suitable for full sun or partial shade, it may grace a lawn or somewhat drier spot. Its summer flowers provide an extra dividend. Clear yellow to orange to red, and sometimes two-toned, with long stamens, they occur in six inch clusters, even on the trunk and main stems. Cylindrical pods to nine inches add interest in autumn. Adaptable to most localities, the tree blooms more abundantly in areas of considerable heat. Outstanding specimens have long adorned the Art Gallery terrace of the Huntington Botanical Gardens in San Marino.

CHIONANTHUS RETUSA | *Oleaceae* | -10°F.
Chinese fringe tree | Late Spring-Summer | China

Four inch clusters of white fringe-like flowers drape branches in late spring. This is one of the most beautiful small deciduous trees growing 20 feet high and often as wide. Two to four inch ovate leaves unfurl before blossoms appear and in fall turn vivid yellow. Though possible in all climate zones except desert and oceanside, *C. retusa* flowers best in sandy loam where several frosts occur in winter and summers are hot.

CHORISIA SPECIOSA | *Bombacaceae* | 27°F.
Floss silk tree | Fall-Winter | Brazil

Light orchid-pink, purplish-rose, mulberry and burgundy are color tones that identify the hibiscus-like flowers of the floss silk tree. One color dominates each tree, appearing on the outer ends of the widely separated petals. Usually the petal bases are ivory or white striped, or spotted brown. These variable six inch blossoms burst suddenly from upright, ball-like buds, cover the entire crown gay and spring-like against the dry autumn landscape.

The tree grows fast the first few years, slowing conveniently before reaching 30 to 60 feet. A lance-straight, grass-green trunk turns gray as the tree matures. Usually it is prominently covered with gray thorn-like spines. The light green leaves, with fan-like arrangement of their leaflets, partially or entirely drop from unusual cold, or as bloom appears. A mature specimen at the Bel Air Hotel furnishes an unforgettable display. There are a number at the Los Angeles Arboretum and groups of these trees adorn the Los Angeles Civic Center.

*Chorisia insignis* has a larger bottle-shaped trunk and white flowers with creamy centers which later turn brown.

## DOMBEYA CACUMINUM

*Sterculiaceae* — 28°F.
Early Spring — Madagascar

This superb evergreen tree is rare in California gardens. The largest specimens at the Huntington Botanical Gardens in San Marino are 50 feet high after 25 years' growth. Plants are narrow in outline, usually with single trunks, and have large maple-like leaves. The hanging clusters of clear rosy pink two inch flowers fall before drying. Flowering begins when plants are mature but if propagated from flowering wood cuttings they will bloom much sooner. The species is being slowly distributed through cuttings and seeds from the Huntington plants.

More common and very different is *Dombeya X cayeuxii* (pink snowball), a hybrid often erroneously identified as *D. acutangula* or *D. wallichii*. It is a much-branched shrub or small tree to 20 feet with hydrangea-like hanging clusters of smaller pink flowers that appear late in spring and are more frost tender than *D. cacuminum*. After flowering the clusters dry brown and remain hanging on the plant unless removed. It is best to prune this *Dombeya* annually in early summer to prevent top-heavy growth. A large specimen can be seen by the Art Gallery terrace at Huntington Gardens.

*Dombeya rotundifolia* comes from South Africa, grows to 30 feet and has white blossoms. It withstands temperatures down to 25°F.

| GREVILLEA ROBUSTA | *Proteaceae* | 20°F. |
|---|---|---|
| Silk oak | Summer | Australia |

Comb-like six to ten inch tresses of orange-yellow flowers and coarsely fern-like leaves, deep olive-green above and silver beneath, distinguish the so-called silk oak, which is not an oak and in no way resembles our oaks. One of the largest imported evergreen trees, 50 to 100 feet, this Australian species was introduced over a century ago and is still widely distributed throughout the southern two-thirds of California. Especially appealing as a young nursery plant, it burgeons upward unbelievably fast. Usually pyramidal in youth, its main trunk divides with maturity to develop a curiously free-form, widely variable shape. It is impressively handsome in the background, particularly when flowering full-grown. Easily cultivated in any soil and most exposures, dry or wet, its most rewarding display of blossom is usually seen in interior valleys and even in the lower desert. One of the oldest plantings flanks Euclid Avenue, from Ontario to Upland. Its chief fault is the very brittle branches which often break in heavy wind.

| HARPULLIA ARBOREA | *Sapindaceae* | 27°F. |
|---|---|---|
| Tulipwood tree | Fall through Spring | Australia-Asia |

A lavish display of pendulous orange seed pods identifies this comely Australasian from fall until summer. Each inflated capsule, an inch and a half across, is two-parted, tangerine or yellow outside, bright red within. Jet black seeds peep tentatively from their enclosures to eventually spread the hulls and shine forth. Flowers are inconspicuous. The tree is dark green, round and dense when placed in a sheltered site. Growth is slow and its new tips are tender. Its ultimate height is about 30 feet. Leaves are pinnate composed of four or five pairs of polished leaflets some six inches long. In its native habitat *H. arborea* is valued for its beautifully marked wood used to make fine cabinets. Successful culture requires well-drained soil, protection from prevailing wind, and considerable heat in summer and fall. A splendid tulipwood is located just south of the Mathematical Sciences Building, UCLA.

HYMENOSPORUM FLAVUM — *Pittosporaceae* — 25°F.

Sweetshade — Spring to Summer — Australia

Honey-scented flowers of soft yellow-orange perfume the environs of the sweetshade from mid-spring to mid-summer. This slender, open evergreen of 20 to 40 feet, with shining light green six inch leaves (which drop with sudden cold or erratic watering), thrives in well-drained soil but sulks in windy places. Its widely spaced limbs and smaller branches may be thickened as well as strengthened by frequent pinching and heading back from extreme youth into maturity. All weak limbs should also be removed. It lends light shade and interesting structure to streets or gardens of both coastal and inland sites. Examples may be seen at the Los Angeles Arboretum, where a notable specimen flowers abundantly for many weeks.

JACARANDA MIMOSIFOLIA | *Bignoniaceae* | 25°F.
Jacaranda | Summer | Brazil and Argentina

Perhaps the best known and most widely loved of our flowering trees, the jacaranda is distinguished by its great, loose, clusters of lavender-blue tubular flowers. These smother the entire crown from May into July, then appear lightly and intermittently, often repeating as late as Thanksgiving in warm exposures. Growing rapidly from seed or cuttings, jacaranda reaches 50 feet with maturity. The leaf canopy develops when the main show of flowers is gone, to cast welcome shadow in late summer and fall. The fern-like leaves drop in mid-winter. This tree is easily adapted to most soils and areas. However, it becomes dwarfed by prolonged drought, tends to be floppy with constant wetness, and may fail to flower when placed on the ocean side of buildings near the seashore. A white form is growing at the Los Angeles Arboretum, and two new species, *J. chelonia* and *J. semiserrata*, have been introduced.

| KOELREUTERIA HENRYI (*K. formosana*) | *Sapindaceae* | 22°F. |
|---|---|---|
| Chinese flame tree | Fall | Taiwan |

This tree is famous for its fall display of salmon seed pods rather than for its earlier brief show of yellow flowers. A moderate grower, 20 to 40 feet, this is an ideal flat-topped patio subject for those who want summer shade and filtered winter sunshine. Shining whorls of golden-green, one to two foot, divided leaves, formed of intricate, shallow-toothed, two to four inch leaflets, encircle branch and twig ends. They turn yellow briefly before dropping, usually in late December. Mature trees produce an arresting crown display of papery fruits, each two inches long, in flaming salmon masses as if the tree-top were wreathed with an odd bougainvillea. Except for the immediate seashore and sites of consistent strong wind, this tree is adaptable to most soils and climate zones in subtropical areas.

LAGERSTROEMIA INDICA
Crape myrtle

*Lythraceae* 10°F.
Summer or Early Fall China

A slow-growing deciduous tree 10 to 35 feet tall, the crape myrtle is best remembered for its late-summer profusion of showy flowers in electric rose pink, crimson, burgundy, shell pink, lavender, or white. The smooth slender trunk is especially beautiful, intricately and delicately mottled gray, fawn and taupe. The winter skeleton is arrestingly strong and clean. Sometimes the leaves turn conspicuously red and gold in late November.

Crape myrtle is best for the drier, hotter areas—it mildews near the beach, and even well inland during some years. The soil should be well-drained and deeply watered.

A good specimen grows on the east side of Schoenberg Hall, UCLA. The rich display of flowers during the summer and fall and the comparatively small size of the tree have made it effective for street plantings, particularly in the San Fernando and San Gabriel valleys.

MARKHAMIA HILDEBRANDTII | *Bignoniaceae* | 32°F.
--- | --- | ---
 | Summer | Africa

Golden trumpet flowers brighten the dusky crown of this beauty in August. The clustered funnelform blossoms, lemon to orange-yellow sometimes with violet stripes, are slightly suspended in terminal panicles. Bloom may not occur every year. The best show follows a mild, sunny winter. Slow to 30 feet, the tree is slender with rounded top. Leaves are especially handsome, opposite, pinnately compound to 15 inches, of burnished olive green. The new growth is purplish-copper in color. Winter chill further purples the foliage which drops from frost or frigid wind. Best placed in a protected spot with maximum summer heat, this tropical African tree is an interesting addition to the palette of an adventuresome gardener.

| MELALEUCA LINARIIFOLIA | *Myrtaceae* | 25°F. |
|---|---|---|
| Snow-in-summer | Summer | Australia |

Narrowly upright, open and very rapidly growing during its first several years, the crown of this tree alters with maturity to a round-headed form of greater density. Thin pale-beige branchlets with clusters of delicately pointed blue-green leaves form an elegant contrast to the honey-brown papery bark peeling on trunk and older limbs.

At all seasons distinguished by its stylized texture and subtle coloring, *M. linariifolia* becomes truly spectacular during early summer in full bloom, giving the effect of new fallen snow. Completely evergreen, this white bottle brush is happy either in moist lawns or with moderate drought, inland or near the sea. See pages 12, 13, and opposite for other bottle brush types.

*Melaleuca elliptica* has deep red blossoms and grows to 12 feet. *M. longicoma* has orange-red blossoms and grows from eight to ten feet; *M. radula*, five feet, has violet blossoms; *M. steedmanii* has brilliant crimson and gold blossoms and can be used as a ground cover since it tends to remain below three feet. *M. wilsonii* has rosy-purple blossoms and grows to about five feet. *M. ericifolia*, a shrub or small tree with white flowers, tolerates salt spray possibly better than others in this genus.

*Melaleuca styphelioides* and *M. quinquenervia* (sometimes called *M. leucadendra*) are two handsome trees to 40 feet with peeling papery tan to whitish bark and creamy white flowers. *M. styphelioides* has pendulous branches and small prickly leaves.

| METROSIDEROS EXCELSA | *Myrtaceae* | 25°F. |
|---|---|---|
| New Zealand Christmas tree | Spring | New Zealand |

The showy, deep red flowers of the New Zealand Christmas tree are dominated by their prominent stiff stamens, numerous and thread-like. These blossoms occur in clusters that submerge the top and sides of this round-headed evergreen from mid-May through June. The leaves are thick and leathery, shining dark green on young growth, gray and hairy on their undersides with maturity. The tree has never attained great size in California, growing very slowly to 30 feet. By nature it has a multiple trunk, quite bushy in youth. It is definitely a subject for coastal areas, usually at its best in the salty, equable air of the seashore, where it endures incredible wind and exposure, an ideal focal material for beach gardens.

See pages 12, 13, 26 for other bottle brush types.

| PAULOWNIA TOMENTOSA (*P. imperialis*) | *Scrophulariaceae* | 15°F. |
| --- | --- | --- |
| Royal paulownia, empress tree | Early Spring | China |

Large-leaved, deciduous, and suggestive of catalpa, the empress tree is Chinese in origin and very old in the history of gardens. It is widely distributed and often naturalized in warmer parts of temperate zones. Forty feet or more tall with sometimes greater spread, it grows rapidly and casts deep shade in summer. Surface roots discourage many ground covers. Vigorous limbs branch low from the trunk or trunks and often curve heavily downward. Leaves are broadly ovate to a foot long, roughly heart-shaped or three-lobed, light to vivid green with beige pubescence covering the underside. They scorch in hottest sun. Furry, light brown buds in panicles to one foot high form in the fall adding interest to the strong-boughed, leafless skeleton. Flowering can be spectacular in early spring unless extremely low temperatures freeze the buds, or near frost causes blossoms to drop before opening. Two inch funnelform flowers, lavender outside, spotted purple and streaked yellow within, crowd the upright panicles. The candelabra-like inflorescence usually precedes new foliage. Persistent two inch seed pods, formed the previous season, accompany the flower show. Best placed away from strong wind, paulownia prefers deep sandy loam.

*P. fargesii* and *P. fortunei* have similar growth, culture, and blooming patterns except flowers tend to be larger and the plants will stand lower temperatures.

| PRUNUS CAMPANULATA | *Rosaceae* | 23°F. |
|---|---|---|
| Taiwan cherry | Spring | Taiwan |

By far the most successful of the many flowering cherries for subtropical landscapes, this one will blossom reasonably well in sight of the ocean. It apparently has little chilling requirement compared to other flowering cherries and tolerates cool summers. Inland it is spectacular. Just as the flowers of fruiting almond begin to shatter, this cherry bursts into strong color, a penetrating cerise, for several weeks, usually in early February. A vigorous tree to some 20 feet, the Taiwan cherry shows bronze new growth while still in blossom. The bell-like little flowers are clustered along arching or pendent branches. Leaves are oblong-oval, usually doubly serrate, glabrous above and below. It is unfortunately scarce in nurseries.

(*Acacia baileyana* is in the left background, see pages 36 and 37).

STENOCARPUS SINUATUS — *Proteaceae* — 27°F.
Firewheel or Rotary tree — Fall-Spring — Australia

This remarkable evergreen tree derives its common name from the shape and color of its flower clusters. The two to three inch scarlet-and-yellow flowers are arranged so they resemble a wheel of flame. The Rotary Club of Sydney, Australia, adopted this tree because the wheel-shaped flowers resemble the Rotary emblem. Southern California Rotary Clubs are following this lead, starting their own plantings of the Rotary tree in public parks. The green buds turn yellow, then open red intermittently throughout the year. Usually a peak display occurs in the heat of early fall. The eight to twelve inch rigid leaves are also showy, shiny dark green and leathery, resembling leaves of some evergreen oaks. The tree is rather narrow and often dense, slow growing to 25 feet. It seems to prefer a well-drained acid soil, deep slow watering and a somewhat sheltered location with excellent air circulation. Chelated nutrients may be needed to correct occasional leaf yellowing in young plants. There is a fine specimen at the Los Angeles Arboretum.

| THEVETIA THEVETIOIDES | *Apocynaceae* | 27°F. |
|---|---|---|
| Giant thevetia | Summer-Fall | Mexico |

In southern California, this plant usually takes the form of a large shrub or shrubby tree, but in the mountains of Mexico between Puebla and Oaxaca it has been seen growing in a dry river bed as a single-trunk, 15 to 20 foot tree. It blooms at intervals during the summer and fall with large open trumpet-like flowers in clusters. Its narrow glossy leaves with a pebbly surface persist through the winter.

*T. peruviana (T. nereifolia)*, yellow oleander, also grows as a large shrub or small tree with evergreen narrow smooth leaves and smaller yellow or apricot-colored funnel-shaped flowers for about four months during the warm season. Both of these species thrive equally well inland and near the coast. The yellow oleander is well-suited to the Palm Springs area.

TABEBUIA CHRYSOTRICHA | *Bignoniaceae* | 24°F.
Golden trumpet tree | Winter or Spring | Brazil

This brown-barked, low-headed and rather open and wide-spreading deciduous tree creates a sensation following a winter cold snap with tight clusters of large golden yellow flowers in dazzling profusion.

The mature leaves which follow the blossoms are composed of three to five leaflets of unequal size, dark green and conspicuously veined above, rough-textured pale olive beneath. Twigs and branches also display an interesting detail of matted beige hairs that suggest thin flocking. This elegant tree promises significant ornamentation for moist or slightly dry sites in areas which have the necessary heat build-up. Near the coast cooler temperatures may prevent heavy blooming.

TABEBUIA IMPETIGINOSA | *Bignoniaceae* | 24°F.
(*T. ipe, T. avellanedae*)
Ipe | Spring | Tropical America

This flamboyant trumpet tree has delicate lavender-pink flowers with yellow centers. Blossoms erupt suddenly to cover bare branches in early spring like a host of pastel butterflies. The plant described as *T. avellanedae* var. *paulensis* has smaller flowers of the same color as *T. impetiginosa,* does not grow as tall, and blooms twice a year. Ipe seems best suited to inland areas.

*Tabebuia chrysotricha*

TIPUANA TIPU — *Leguminosae* — 25°F.

Tipu tree — Summer — So. Brazil, Argentina

Abundant sprays of apricot to yellow pea-shaped blossoms drip from masses of light green fern-like foliage from early to mid-summer. The tipu is hardy and fast-growing, its flat-topped head often spreading wider than its height, which varies from 25 to 30 feet. Particularly suited to inland summers, this tree furnishes filtered shade for ten months, losing its leaves briefly in mid-winter. Its pliable limbs may easily be thinned to produce an extremely open structure, or shortened to achieve greater density and less diameter. It grows easily in most watered soils.

There is a notable avenue planting along Colby, from Gateway to National, in West Los Angeles. Old specimens may be seen at the Los Angeles Country Club entrance on Wilshire Boulevard and in Elysian Park.

(Bougainvillea in foreground of illustration, see page 100).

# MAGNOLIA

## Flowering Trees and Shrubs

*Magnoliaceae*

*Michelia doltsopa*

Many outstanding flowering trees belong to the magnolia family. Probably best known are the evergreen and deciduous members of the genus *Magnolia*. Less well known are the evergreen trees in the genera *Michelia* and *Talauma*. Since the members of this family are native to regions of high rainfall, when cultivated in hot inland areas of southern California they do best with light afternoon shade with their roots protected by a mulch or ground cover.

Most tolerant of heat and dry conditions is the southern evergreen magnolia, *M. grandiflora*, with large glossy leaves and showy flowers; 'Majestic Beauty' is one of its better cultivars. Another evergreen species is *M. delavayi* from China, a rare but handsome-foliaged background tree.

Among the deciduous species which bloom earlier and more spectacularly, the best is *M.* X *soulangeana*, with its many cultivars, all large shrubs or small trees covered with white to purplish flowers early in the year. *M. kobus stellata* forms a dense shrub with smaller but profuse white flowers. Especially elegant in form and color of bloom are *M. denudata*, *M. liliflora* 'Nigra' and *M. sargentiana robusta*.

| MICHELIA DOLTSOPA | *Magnoliaceae* | 25°F. |
|---|---|---|
| | Spring | Asia |

Five to seven inch cream-white flowers adorn this 20 foot evergreen tree. From fat brown velvet buds, flowers open satin-like and fragrant, suggestive of magnolia. As early as Christmas they cover the tree, remaining as late as April against shining deep green leaves which are thin, leather-like and three to eight inches long. Tall in its native Himalayas, it remains somewhat shrubby in the subtropics, upright, and close-limbed. Rich, leafy soil well-aerated, some wind protection and a cool, moist root-run are recommended.

Acacia baileyana

# ACACIA

## Flowering Trees and Shrubs

*Leguminosae*

The golden glory of acacia trees blooming from mid-winter through spring invariably attracts the admiration of visitors to California, perhaps because of their airy beauty or, perhaps, because this is the only state where they are grown in any number.

There are approximately 800 species of *Acacia* described from the warmer parts of the world, about half of them from Australia. Of these, perhaps 100 have been tried in California and fewer than 50 are available in the nurseries. We have scarcely scratched the surface of their potential.

Most of the species that have been introduced here are from dry areas and are well adapted to poor soil, little water and less care. They languish in lawns or watered gardens. There are species, however, that will take garden conditions and some that must have water. Most acacias need sun and fast drainage but there are some which prefer partial shade and some that will take heavy clay. Some of these preferences are indicated for the acacias listed in the Calendar of Acacia Flowering. Most of the acacias that are available here are frost tolerant but the majestic *A. elata* is tender when young.

Acacias are said to have two serious faults. They are short-lived and their branches are brittle and easily broken by the wind, both faults that can be mitigated by proper culture. An acacia planted in the location to which it is best adapted, watered to encourage deep rooting, and pruned and properly staked to strengthen its trunk will often outlast its normal life-expectancy.

The low, shrubby acacias which are most promising for the average home garden have hardly been tried. Their small size, compact shape and long blooming periods make them desirable and many of them adapt well to garden conditions. A few species are available at nurseries. The keen gardener who wants to try some of the others can easily grow them from seed—using the boiling water method to break down the hard seed coat. Many of them will grow rapidly and bloom in 18 months.

ACACIA BAILEYANA | *Leguminosae* | 20°F.
Bailey's acacia | Winter | Australia

This is a fast growing 20 to 30 foot tree for rather dry slopes and well-drained soil. With the New Year *Acacia baileyana* bursts into a fluffy cloud of clear yellow fragrant flowers displayed against the blue-gray head of fern-like evergreen foliage. See page 29 for another illustration of *A. baileyana*. A distinguished, much rarer variation with purple-tinged foliage is *A. baileyana* 'Purpurea.'

*A. glandulicarpa*, one of the best shrub acacias, is a compact mass of green most of the year. In spring it turns into a golden ball seven to eight feet tall and broad with tiny puff-ball, delightfully fragrant flower clusters. This species as well as *A. lineata*, *A. gladiiformis*, *A. cardiophylla*, *A. cultriformis* and others are useful shrubs for slopes or freeway embankments. See the bloom chart on the next page.

*Acacia glandulicarpa*

# ACACIAS CAN PROVIDE COLOR ALL YEAR

With judicious selection of species one may have acacia bloom every month of the year. The following chart may aid in choosing the acacias which will bloom when a garden plan most needs color. It should be kept in mind, however, that many of the acacias bloom erratically or intermittently through the year and cannot be held strictly to the time-table.

S *A. calamifolia,* 8′ to 12′ shrub, needle-like leaves, bright yellow flowers
S *A. cardiophylla,* 10′ to 15′ shrub, arching branches, bright yellow flowers
*A. cultriformis,* shrub to 15′, silvery gray leaves, yellow flowers
*A. cyanophylla,* 20′ tree, bluish leaves, orange flowers
FS *A. dealbata,* 50′ tree, long-lived, yellow-gold flowers
FS *A. decurrens,* 40′ tree, dark green leaves, bright yellow flowers
*A. elata,* 60′ tree, long-lived, dark green leaves, creamy flowers, blooming variable
FS *A. karroo,* 20′ tree from South Africa, rich green leaves, yellow flowers
*A. longifolia,* often sold as *A. latifolia,* 20′ shrub or tree, golden flower spikes
FS *A mearnsii (A. decurrens mollis).* 40′ tree, creamy flowers
*A. pendula,* 25′ tree, slow, blue-gray leaves, weeping, blooming variable
FS *A. podalyriaefolia,* 20′ shrub or tree, silvery gray leaves, light yellow flowers
W *A. pruinosa,* 60′ tree, coppery new growth, pale yellow flowers
F *A. pubescens,* 15′ shrub, feathery leaves, graceful, drooping branches
*A. pycnantha,* 25′ tree, light green leaves, golden yellow flowers
F *A. retinodes,* often sold as *A. floribunda,* 20′ tree, blooms most of year near coast
W *A. riceana,* 20′ tree, prefers coastal conditions, weeping, pale yellow flowers
S *A. saligna,* 20′ tree, weeping, vivid yellow large flowers
*A. sieberiana woodii,* 30′ flat-topped tree from South Africa, pale cream flowers
FW *A. subporosa,* 40′ tree, pendent chains of whitish flowers
*A. verticillata,* 20′ shrub or tree, conifer-like, pale yellow flower spikes
*A. vestita,* 10′ shrub or tree, weeping, ashen gray leaves, beautiful tub plant

*Low shrubby acacias*

S *Acacia acinacea*, 3′-6′, pale yellow, takes heavy soils
S *A. alata,* 5′, partial shade, leafless, pale yellow flowers
S *A. obliqua,* 4′, arching branches, yellow flowers, takes heavy soils
FS *A. rupicola*, 5′, showy all winter

Jan Feb Mar Apr May Jun Jul Aug Sep Oct Nov Dec

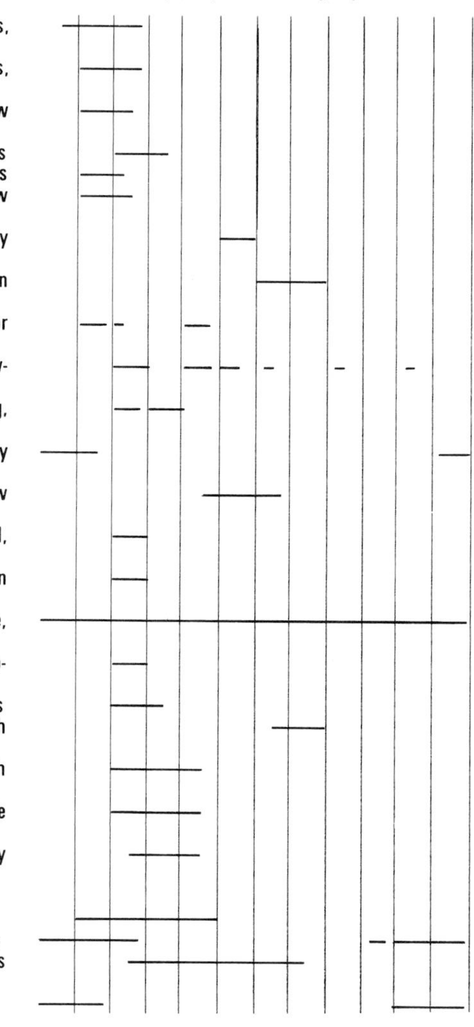

Note: S=especially showy; F=fragrant; W=water regularly

# CASSIA
## Flowering Trees and Shrubs

*Leguminosae*

*Cassia carnaval*

Cassias are another large group of trees and shrubs which will provide a wealth of yellow for the landscape practically all year if the bloom period of the species is carefully noted.

| CASSIA CARNAVAL | *Leguminosae* | 26°F. |
|---|---|---|
| Crown of gold tree | Fall | Argentina |

Pictured above is *Cassia carnaval,* considered by some a variant of *C. excelsa.* This partially evergreen tree displays abundant 12 to 16 inch up-thrust spikes of bright yellow flowers at the ends of the light green branch tips, usually in very late summer or early fall.

It grows rapidly to 40 feet and thrives in full sun with fairly fast-draining, warm soil, in somewhat wind-protected locations. It is tender when young, but has tolerated 26°F. when mature. It needs moisture during the growing season and should be pruned hard after flowering.

*Cassia multijuga* from Brazil is an upright tree with smaller leaves and very long flower spikes of clear yellow which appear in September and October. *C. liebmanii* from Mexico is a pagoda-shaped tree to 20 feet, blooming twice a year with flowers somewhat smaller than *C. carnaval.*

*Cassia leptophylla* (above), the gold medallion tree from Brazil, blooms in the summer, and has exceptional beauty. It is open-headed, low-spreading and near-evergreen with fern-like foliage. Branch ends produce a spectacle of six to eight inch golden yellow clusters, brilliant for several weeks. This species is perhaps the most shapely and graceful of the cassias in California. Like all other cassias, it grows fast to its mature height of 30 feet.

*Cassia leptophylla* (opposite)

Many cassias are attractive shrubs. Among the most popular is *Cassia artemisioides* (below), a silvery, almost needle-leafed shrub with bright buttercup yellow flowers. It attains a height of four to six feet, needs good drainage and blooms several times a year. It is useful for the small garden and grows well in desert areas. It must not be over-watered. *Cassia surattensis* var. *suffruticosa*, native to tropical Asia and Polynesia, is one of the most prolific blooming shrubs, providing a mass of color from June to November and forming a dense mass to eight feet high and about as wide. When grown in rich sandy loam in full sun or very light shade and given ample moisture, it offers a very lush green tropical appearance. In cooler areas it may become partially deciduous and will suffer frost damage below 23°F. Plants will flower the second or third year from seed. *C. cocquimbensis* is a 12 foot shrub from Chile which blooms in spring and again in the fall, with dense clusters of one and a half-inch flowers. Other desirable shrub cassias are *C. alata* (tender), *C. bicapsularis* (tall and winter blooming), *C. nemophila*, *C. corymbosa*, *C. helmsii*, *C. biflora*, and *C. chatelaineana*.

*Cassia artemisioides*

# THE REMARKABLE EUCALYPTUS

## Flowering Trees and Shrubs

*Myrtaceae*

The California landscape would look strange indeed without the familiar eucalyptus, introduced in large numbers from Australia in the 19th century, when a frenzied 'eucalyptus boom' promoted their use as railroad ties and other commercial products.

The genus, a member of the myrtle family, comprises over 600 species, native to Australia, nearby islands, and Indomalaysia. All are evergreen and characterized by a bud-cap or operculum which pops off to reveal the beauty of a flower made up mostly of stamens. Species vary from five foot shrubs to forest giants of 300 feet or more occurring in such varied climatic conditions as tropical rain-forests, winter snows in high mountains, deserts and Mediterranean-type climates.

When many Californians hear the word 'eucalyptus' they are apt to think of the earliest and most common species introduced, the Tasmanian blue gum, *Eucalyptus globulus,* with its giant 100 to 200 foot stature, ever-shedding bark and greedy roots. This one is useful as a wind-break but its white flowers are inconspicuous and it is not suitable for urban landscaping. If a tall eucalyptus is desired, *E. citriodora* with smooth, white trunks and lemon-scented leaves is recommended.

This book, however, is concerned primarily with those species of eucalyptus having showy flowers, many of which are native to the semi-arid regions of southwestern Australia. Most are small in stature, bloom over periods of two to three months or more and sometimes several times a year. Flowers come in a wide range of colors including red, pink, yellow, orange, green, cream and mauve. The blossoms make showy floral arrangements, keeping for a week or more in water when the cut ends of stems are split. Many of these colorful species are recent introductions and have not yet received the attention they deserve from the nursery or floral industries, landscape architects and home-owners. These plants are not 'messy' and make ideal small trees for the home garden. Their cultivation is simple and most of them will tolerate average garden conditions provided they have good drainage and are not over-watered. They thrive both in coastal and inland areas and will tolerate temperatures down to the mid-twenties, except for *E. ficifolia* which may be injured by temperatures below 27°F.

It is difficult to place some *Eucalyptus* species into tree or shrub categories. Many are intermediate. In addition to the four species described and illustrated on pages 46, 47, 48, and 49, the following are worthy of attention.

*Eucalyptus*

X *rhodantha*

Species to be planted for winter-flowering are *E. preissiana,* a 10 to 15 foot shrub or small tree with large yellow flowers; *E.* X 'Torwood,' a natural hybrid of *E. torquata* and *E. woodwardii,* originating in Western Australia, a 10 to 15 foot tree with dark yellow or orange-colored flowers; *E. tetraptera,* a shrubby tree with flowers having a large four-sided red flower base and red stamens; and *E. pyriformis,* a shrubby tree with large flowers in colors varying from red or pink to cream.

Some species bloom not only primarily in winter but at intervals throughout the year. Among these are *E. forrestiana* and *E. stoatei,* both small trees with flowers with a red flower base and yellow stamens, resembling small Chinese lanterns; *E. kruseana* reaches 20-30 feet and has pale yellow, almost white flowers and small round silvery leaves; and *E. orbifolia,* a 15 to 20 foot shrubby tree with round silvery leaves and clusters of creamy-yellow flowers.

Winter and spring flowering eucalyptus include *E. caesia,* a 15 to 20 foot tree with pink flowers; *E. macrocarpa,* a four to six foot shrub with large silvery leaves and large three inch red flowers; *E.* X *orpetii* (page 45), a natural hybrid between *E. caesia* and *E. macrocarpa,* which shows considerable variation in the seedlings as to flower size and color as well as leaf shape and color, with all the variants attractive shrubs; and *E. megacornuta,* a 15 to 25 foot tree with a single trunk and clusters of large green flowers.

A summer flowering species, *E. calophylla rosea,* resembling *E. ficifolia* (page 48) in size, shape and flower color, is attractive also for its bronze-pink new foliage. *E. macrandra,* a 15 to 20 foot tree with single or multiple trunks, bears clusters of small yellow flowers from summer into fall. If the cut flowers are dried before the stamens fall, they make attractive dry arrangements. *E. woodwardii,* 10 to 15 feet tall and somewhat rangy with silvery leaves and bright yellow flowers, blooms primarily in fall and winter.

Some species of *Eucalyptus* flower intermittently throughout the year and flowers may be found in almost any month. Among these are *E.* X *rhodantha* (page 43), a four to eight foot shrub with large round leaves and red flowers; *E. torquata,* a 10 to 15 foot tree with showy clusters of small coral-red flowers; and *E.* X 'Helen Ayres,' developed in California by Helen Ayres, a hybrid between *E. rhodantha* and *E. woodwardii.* One specimen, after seven years, attained a height of about 15 feet. It has short-stemmed oval leaves and large red flowers. Possibly other seedlings of this cross will show interesting variations in flower color and leaf structure.

*Eucalyptus X orpetii*

EUCALYPTUS SIDEROXYLON | *Myrtaceae* | 20°F.
Red iron bark | Winter or Spring | Australia

There are two forms of this eucalyptus. One is quite pendulous, often weeping to the ground at maturity; the other is more upright, its foliage slightly greener. Both of these evergreens can attain 40 feet and have persistent red-brown bark and gray-green leaves that partially color mahogany in cold weather. The tough light branches drape themselves with skeins of fragile rose-pink to red blossoms which appear intermittently from autumn to spring. Both grow fast in a wide range of soils and microclimates from beach to desert. They are resistant to most wind with little pruning, and are seldom subject to disease or insects.

EUCALYPTUS ERYTHROCORYS — *Myrtaceae* — 25°F.
Red cap gum — Fall and at intervals — Western Australia

The three inch chartreuse to golden-yellow flowers of this eucalyptus are borne in heavy clusters and emerge from buds covered with a bright scarlet cap. Its polished bright green leaves are long, rather thick, and variably shaped. The seed capsules are heavy and attractive. Unlike many species of eucalyptus, *E. erythrocorys* tolerates summer watering where there is reasonable drainage.

This eucalyptus may be grown with either single or multiple trunks and can attain 30 feet. It is clean, hardy, and fast-growing, blooming a month or more at a time at least three times a year. The cut flowers and buds arrange effectively and last well. The species is conspicuous in groups near the west end of the demonstration gardens at the Los Angeles Arboretum.

| EUCALYPTUS FICIFOLIA | *Myrtaceae* | 28 °F. |
|---|---|---|
| Flame eucalyptus | Summer or Any Season | Western Australia |

This eucalyptus varies in blossom color from pure crimson to scarlet, orange, salmon, pink, white and yellow green. Selected color forms are available. The flowers average two inches across and occur in large clusters like tight bouquets, rather evenly spaced over the rounded crown of leathery dark green leaves. The bark is dark, furrowed and persistent. The tree grows slowly to 35 feet with similar spread. The cut flowers are effective indoors, as are the large gray-brown woody seed pods. At its best within a few miles of the ocean, *E. ficifolia* dislikes wet, slowly-draining soil. It is a favorite subject for lining avenues. Such a spectacle may be viewed intermittently along Alma Real in Pacific Palisades.

| | | |
|---|---|---|
| EUCALYPTUS LEUCOXYLON MACROCARPA 'ROSEA' | *Myrtaceae* | 22 °F. |
| Dwarf white ironbark | Summer and Fall | Australia |

This brilliant-flowered variety to 25 feet tall is smaller than the long-cultivated species known as white ironbark. An attractive white trunk and long-pointed leaves add to its charm. Free and variable in form, it retains the subtle coloring of its better-known relative, but is more widely adapted to urban planting and far more showy in blossom. The tree may bloom when only three years old, the abundantly massed flowers a clear, deep red. Easily at home in most California soils, it usually blooms well either inland or near the coast.

*Erythrina coralloides*

# ERYTHRINA
## The Coral Trees and Shrubs

*Leguminosae*

Of all the flowering trees growing in the City of Los Angeles, the coral trees, or erythrinas, official flowering trees for the City, are among the most spectacular. These trees have been ornamentals in Mexico since Aztec days and their use in Los Angeles reflects its colorful Mexican heritage.

Coral trees are members of the pea family (Leguminosae) and have pea-like blossoms in various modified forms. The hundred or more erythrinas are native of relatively cool and dry tropical and subtropical areas in all continents. To fit each of southern California's microclimates, 15 or more species are now cultivated, and more will be available as testing establishes their adaptability.

Some coral trees are best for mild coastal areas, while others are hardy in inland areas. Some are shrubby, others are large shade trees of 40 feet or more. Some are suitable as street trees, others for parkway planting or as landscape specimens. Some are evergreen, others are deciduous with an interesting structure of bare branches.

*Erythrina* is from the Greek for red, but flowers vary from pink through crimson, scarlet and burnt orange. The blooming period lasts four to six weeks or longer, and different species bloom at different seasons.

Perhaps the most colorful and one of the hardier coral trees is *Erythrina coralloides* (naked coral or cone flame tree), native of Mexico (illustrated opposite). The blossoms are clustered on the ends of branches like crimson candles. There is also a pink form. For about six weeks between March and May the tree is without leaves. The tree seldom exceeds 20 feet and the branches bend down, requiring judicious pruning. There are fine specimens along Santa Monica Boulevard in Beverly Hills, along Westwood Boulevard at UCLA and at the Huntington Botanical Gardens. A flame tree forest of over a thousand of this and of three other species was planted by the Camp Fire Girls in Harbor Park, Los Angeles, in 1962 in celebration of their 50th anniversary.

The shrubby corals include *Erythrina* X *bidwillii* a hybrid of *Erythrina crista-galli* and *Erythrina herbacea* (Florida coral bean). It is an exceedingly handsome plant attaining a height of three to six feet, is useful for the small garden, withstands severe frost and can bloom from April to November. The spikes of red flowers should be cut back after blooming. Bidwill's erythrina may be seen at the Union Oil Center, Los Angeles, and the Huntington Gardens.

*Erythrina humeana*, Natal coral, (picture on page 52), a native of South Africa, produces red-orange spikes of penetrating brilliance terminating the branches while this coral is still a three foot sprout. The flowers are primarily produced in the autumn but in a hot location specimens have been known to bloom almost constantly and copiously from

*Erythrina* X *bidwillii*

*Erythrina humeana*

late June to December. Natal coral may reach 30 feet in height and it is suggested that multiple trunks trained to staggered heights can keep many flowers in easy view. This is one of the deciduous erythrinas and the branches are bare for two or more of the winter months, but it possesses interesting structure. It always requires well-drained soil and in cooler areas should be placed in protected positions. A fine specimen can be seen at the Los Angeles Arboretum. It has been suggested that the plant which we call *Erythrina humeana* is probably a hybrid between *E. humeana*, primarily a shrub in South Africa, and *E. princeps*. In Africa the shrub form is sometimes designated *E. humeana* var. *raja*. The variety *raja*, a shrub to some ten feet, may be seen in the UCLA Botanical Garden.

Clusters of brilliant red sickle-shaped flowers in the spring and moderate frost tolerance make *Erythrina falcata* (illustrated page 53), a large evergreen tree, a valuable addition to the southern California landscape. Although it may not bloom for 15 years or more when grown from seed, it blooms much sooner when grown from cuttings of wood from mature trees. The tree has an upright habit of growth and may attain a height of at least 50 feet, making it a striking subject for specimen plantings. A pink flowered variant is occasionally found. Large specimens may be seen at the South Coast Botanic Garden, at the Los Angeles Arboretum, and in Plummer Park in West Hollywood.

*Erythrina lysistemon* (kaffirboom) illustrated on page 54 is another valuable introduction from South Africa. An almost evergreen tree with rounded crown, it may grow to 40 feet. Slender red blossoms fold back against the stem in late winter and early spring while the tree is essentially leafless. Kaffirboom is frost-tender and best suited to coastal areas and inland to downtown Los Angeles. Fine specimens may be seen on the UCLA campus.

One of southern California's best known avenue plantings is that of *Erythrina caffra* (coast kaffirboom) on San Vicente Boulevard from Brentwood to the ocean. This tree is also spectacular at Corona del Mar (front cover picture), in MacArthur Park, and many other locations. The coast kaffirboom, a native of South Africa, can reach 80 feet. It is usually smaller in southern California, but still a large, spreading tree with usually flattened crown not suited to small gardens. The trees are deciduous for a short time before flowering and the bare branch structure is attractive. Clusters of large, wide-open, scarlet flowers appear in late winter and early spring. The tree is resistant to oak root fungus.

*Erythrina americana* (colorín), native of Mexico, long cultivated in Europe, Hawaii and the West Indies, is a small upright tree to about 25 feet and hardy to at least 25°F. In Mexico City it is planted as a street tree, and is common on the campus of the University of Mexico. The tree is usually deciduous in winter, although in protected areas near the ocean it may be evergreen. The red flowers appear in the spring, and are sold in Latin America markets for salads.

Another hardy, deciduous coral tree is *Erythrina crista-galli* (cockscomb tree) from Brazil. It may bloom in spring, fall, and irregularly during summer, with showy erect, pink to red flowers. The flowering branches die back after blooming. They may be pruned to the stubby trunk of the 15 foot tree.

*Erythrina acanthocarpa* (tambookie thorn), native of South Africa, is a spiny bush about four feet high and well adapted to the small garden. This deciduous species tolerates considerable cold. Its scarlet flowers with greenish-yellow tips are breathtaking for three or four weeks in spring.

*Erythrina sandwicensis*, a 25 to 30 foot tree native of Hawaii, is somewhat frost-tender. Showy masses of red to salmon-colored, sometimes white, flowers appear in spring. This tree is probably limited to the immediate warm coastal areas.

An erythrina grown here for a number of years is *E. latissima* from Africa, a small tree

*Erythrina falcata*

Erythrina lysistemon

with very corky bark.

A number of other erythrinas are being tested. In many cases the identifications have not been verified and they are being grown with the names under which they were introduced. Some introductions from gardens in Australia and Chile are apparently hybrids with *E. falcata* as one parent. Many species of coral trees, largely of Central American origin, have been received from Dr. B.A. Krukoff, international authority on the genus *Erythrina*, and these are being grown in a number of sites throughout the city. Some have not withstood frost damage, but some appear promising, among them *Erythrina guatemalensis*. It is probable that new introductions will be made from these and others to add to our already rich collection of coral trees.

Coral trees are easy to grow, rooting readily from cuttings, and require little attention. Most important is selection of the species hardy in your area. Most coral trees are rapid growers and space must be allowed for the often spreading rounded crowns of the tree species. They should not be over-watered and, as with most plants, good drainage is important. The trees flower best if deliberately dried off for a short period before formation of flower buds. Any pruning necessary to shape the crown should be done after blooming to avoid cutting away the next year's flower buds. Exceptions to the little pruning rule are *Erythrina crista-galli*, which dies back to its main branches in the fall, with blossoms forming on new wood; and *Erythrina* X *bidwillii*, which forms new flowering branches each spring.

# ADDITIONAL FLOWERING TREES OF MERIT

| Species | Family | Common Name | Origin | Height to | Color | Season of Color | Hardy to |
|---|---|---|---|---|---|---|---|
| **Evergreen Trees** | | | | | | | |
| Acmena smithii | Myrtaceae | lili pili tree | Australia | 25′ | orchid pink berries | winter | 20°F. |
| Agonis juniperina | Myrtaceae | juniper myrtle | Australia | 25′-35′ | white | summer & fall | 27°F. |
| Angophora costata | Myrtaceae | gum myrtle | Australia | 40′-50′ | white | summer | 25°F. |
| Arbutus unedo | Ericaceae | strawberry tree | So. Europe | 20′-30′ | white fls., red fruit | fall & winter | 28°F. |
| Brassaia actinophylla | Araliaceae | Queensland umbrella tree | Australia | 20′ | green, turning red | summer | 25°F. |
| Caesalpinia spinosa | Leguminosae | | Cuba & So. America | 12′ | yellow-red | winter-spring | 20°F. |
| Chiranthodendron pentadactylon | Sterculiaceae | monkey hand tree | Mexico | 40′-50′ | deep red | March-October | 27°F. |
| Clethra arborea | Clethraceae | lily of the valley tree | Madeira | 20′ | white | late summer | 24°F. |
| Crinodendron dependens | Elaeocarpaceae | lily of the valley tree | Chile | 25′ | white fls., cream & flame seed pods | summer & fall | 22°F. |
| Cunonia capensis | Cunoniaceae | African red alder | So. Africa West Indies | 25′ | white | summer | 20°F. |
| Drimys winteri | Magnoliaceae | **winter's bark** | So. America | 25′ | creamy white | spring | 20°F. |
| Hakea laurina | Proteaceae | sea urchin tree | Australia | 30′ | cream & red | fall & winter | 20°F. |
| Harpephyllum caffrum | Anacardiaceae | kaffir plum | So. Africa | 35′ | red fruit | winter | 25°F. |
| Lagunaria patersonii | Malvaceae | primrose tree | Australia | 40′ | pale rose | summer | 25°F. |
| Pittosporum phillyraeoides | Pittosporaceae | **weeping pittosporum** | Australia | 20′ | yellow | spring | 25°F. |
| P. rhombifolium | | **Queensland pittosporum** | Australia | 35′ | showy orange fruit | fall & winter | 25°F. |
| P. undulatum | | Victorian box | Australia | 40′ | white | spring | 25°F. |
| Pyrus kawakamii | Rosaceae | evergreen pear | Taiwan | 30′ | white | winter & spring | 20°F. |
| Rhodosphaera rhodanthema | Anacardiaceae | yellow-wood | Australia | 70′ | red | spring | 28°F. |
| Robinsonella cordata | Malvaceae | blue hibiscus tree | Guatemala | 20′ | violet blue | spring | 25°F. |
| Schinus terebinthifolius | Anacardiaceae | Brazilian pepper | Brazil | 30′ | showy red berries | winter | 20°F. |
| Schotia brachypetala | Leguminosae | tree fuchsia | So. Africa | 20′ | crimson | spring | 30°F. |
| S. latifolia | | forest boerboon | So. Africa | 30′ | pink or rose | spring | 30°F. |

| | | | | | | | |
|---|---|---|---|---|---|---|---|
| Schrebera alata | Oleaceae | | So. Africa | 20′ | pink | late spring | 25°F. |
| Sophora secundiflora | Leguminosae | mescal bean | Mexico, New Mexico & Texas | 25′ | violet blue | spring | 17°F. |
| Spathodea campanulata | Bignoniaceae | African tulip tree | Tropical Africa | 70′ | scarlet | late summer & fall | 32°F. |
| Syzygium jambos | Myrtaceae | rose apple | East Indies | 30′ | rosy fruit | fall & winter | 30°F. |
| S. paniculatum | | Australian cherry | Australia | 40′ | greenish-yellow fruit | fall & winter | 26°F. |
| Talauma hodgsonii | Magnoliaceae | | Himalayas | 30′ | creamy white | late spring | 25°F. |
| Tristania conferta | Myrtaceae | Brisbane box | Australia | 60′ | white | summer | 26°F. |
| Virgilia divaricata | Leguminosae | choice tree | So. Africa | 30′ | rosy pink | spring | 25°F. |
| Vitex lucens | Verbenaceae | chaste tree | New Zealand | 30′ | dark red | winter | 25°F. |
| **Deciduous Trees** | | | | | | | |
| Acrocarpus fraxinifolius | Leguminosae | | India | 60′ | scarlet | early spring | 30°F. |
| Aesculus X carnea | Hippocastanaceae | red horse-chestnut | Garden hybrid | 40′ | flesh to rosy pink | spring | 10°F. |
| A. X carnea 'Briotii' | | red horse-chestnut | Garden hybrid | 40′ | rosy crimson | spring | 10°F. |
| Cercis canadensis | Leguminosae | red bud | Eastern U.S. | 30′ | rosy pink | spring | 0°F. |
| C. siliquastrum | | Judas tree | So. Europe | 25′ | rosy pink | spring | 15°F. |
| Cornus florida | Cornaceae | flowering dogwood | Eastern U.S. | 40′ | white, pink or rose | spring | 0°F. |
| C. nuttallii | | western dogwood | Western U.S. | 75′ | white | spring | 15°F. |
| Dais cotinifolia | Thymelaeaceae | pompon tree | So. Africa | 20′ | pink | late spring | 25°F. |
| Davidia involucrata | Nyssaceae | dove tree or handkerchief tree | China | 50′ | white | spring | 0°F. |
| Halesia carolina | Styracaceae | silverbell or snowdrop tree | Southeastern U.S. | 30′ | white | spring | 10°F. |
| Liriodendron tulipifera | Magnoliaceae | American tulip tree | Eastern U.S. | 75′ | green, yellow & orange | summer | 10°F. |
| Melia azedarach | Meliaceae | pride of India | Asia | 50′ | lavender pink | late spring, summer | 10°F. |
| M.a. 'Umbraculifera' | | Texas umbrella tree | | 30′ | pink | late spring, summer | 10°F. |
| Parkinsonia aculeata | Leguminosae | Jerusalem thorn | Tropical America | 30′ | yellow | summer & all year | 15°F. |
| Plumeria rubra acutifolia | Apocynaceae | frangipani | Mexico & W. Indies | 15′ | white | summer & fall | 30°F. |
| Salmalia *(Bombax)* malabarica | Bombacaceae | silk-cotton tree | India, Malaya | 75′ | red | spring | 28°F. |
| Sesbania punicea | Leguminosae | glory pea | Argentina | 12′ | scarlet | spring & summer | 25°F. |

*Solanum rantonnetii,* see page 85

# *Chapter II*

# FLOWERING SHRUBS

In subtropical areas it is possible to have shrubs in bloom throughout the year. Many gardens have room for only a few trees but most can accommodate a variety of shrubs to provide continuous displays of color. It may take several years for a tree to bloom but most shrubs will produce flowers while still young. For this reason and because they are so significant in landscape use they have been subjects for hybridization and selection throughout the ages. Camellias have been grown for their beauty for over 900 years; the Persians had gardens of roses; the ancient Greeks used roses in their wreaths; and in the Roman Republic roses, not medals, were awarded to military heroes. It is little wonder that we now grow hundreds of cultivars of these long-time favorites.

The choice of shrubs is even greater than for trees. The following pages include the true shrubs, woody plants that produce shoots or stems from the base and do not have a single trunk. Many shrub species of *Acacia, Eucalyptus, Magnolia, Cassia,* and *Erythrina* are discussed in the previous chapter. It is not easy to tell a tree from a shrub since some shrubs, with pruning, can make satisfactory small trees and several small trees planted together can produce a shrub effect. Many non-shrubby plants such as strelitzia, poinsettia, aloe, and many succulents can be used in the same way as shrubs. All of these are included in other chapters in this book. Shrubs offer an additional bonus since many of them make ideal cut materials for indoor decorations; others can be grown satisfactorily in containers for the patio.

The final selections for this chapter, while they represent only a fraction of the desirable shrubs suitable for subtropical gardens, are most significant for the wealth of color they can add to the landscape. They have been chosen for their ability to grow easily under average garden conditions in subtropical climates.

Many additional shrubs are described in the chapter on California native plants and others are listed at the end of this chapter. It is impossible in the space available to include all the cultivars and species that may be in the trade. The gardener will find other shrubs in the nurseries and to obtain the flower color desired it is recommended that the selections be made when the plants are in bloom.

*Rhododendron* species and hybrids

| RHODODENDRON | *Ericaceae* | Tender to hardy |
|---|---|---|
| Rhododendron, azalea | Spring | Asia, North America |

Though shrubs commonly called rhododendrons and azaleas both belong to the genus *Rhododendron,* most people refer to the large eight to ten foot evergreen shrubs with five to six inch deep green leaves when they use the term rhododendron, and to the two to four foot evergreen or deciduous forms with smaller leaves and flowers when they use the term azalea. The genus *Rhododendron* contains more than 500 species and innumerable cultivars varying from tiny alpine tufts native to the windswept barrens of Tibet to huge rain forest trees 80 feet tall with shining 32 inch deep green leaves. Native over a wide area they thus show a wide variation as to temperature tolerance.

A few cultivars of the large-leaved group, such as 'Pink Pearl,' are occasionally seen in southern California. The popularity of the smaller leaved azaleas, covered as they often are with a complete mantle of blossoms (see page 59), has increased rapidly. Since they do well in either sun or shade the southern indicas or sun azaleas are used most frequently. Popular cultivars are: 'Pride of Dorking,' cerise red; 'Formosa,' lavender purple; 'George Taber,' orchid pink; 'Southern Charm,' pink; 'Glory of Sunninghill,' orange. The fragrant white cultivar, 'Alaska,' is almost everblooming and needs partial shade. The kurumes do equally well but their flowers are smaller. Less well-known are the satsuki azaleas, distinctive in their late blooming (May and June), very large and variably colored flowers, and relatively low, compact growth. Some of those that thrive in southern California are 'Gumpo,' white; 'Pink Gumpo,' rose-pink; 'Gunbi,' large single light pink; 'Geisha Girl,' single rose-red; 'Kagetsu Muji,' large, single white; 'Shinnyo-No-Tsuki,' magenta with white centers; and 'Eikan,' white, variegated pink.

Recently species of the section *Vireya,* popularly called Malesian rhododendrons, have been introduced. These show great promise for areas with warm summers and frost-free winters, for they may be damaged below 28°F. but withstand summer heat if lightly shaded. They are unusual in flower shape, often startling in their colors, and may bloom several times yearly. Some successfully grown outdoors at Huntington Gardens are: *R. laetum* and *R. aurigeranum,* with clear yellow flowers; *R. zoelleri,* a striking orange-yellow; and *R. jasminiflorum,* with tubular white flowers reminiscent of *Daphne.* All but the last are from New Guinea. Two excellent hybrids of this group are *R. phaeopeplum* X *R. lochae,* with fragrant flowers of an unusual pink, and *R. wrightianum* X *R. lochae,* with compact growth and small, pendent, ruby-red tubular flowers.

For all types of *Rhododendron,* planting soil must be loose, high in humus and slightly acid. Good drainage is a must. Some growers recommend planting in raised beds of nursery soil mix to assure good drainage, and the use of an insulating mulch. With the alkaline soils and waters of the southwest, iron deficiency chlorosis can be a problem unless iron chelates are used. Occasional applications of soil sulfur will help maintain the proper soil acidity.

| BRUNFELSIA CALYCINA FLORIBUNDA | *Solanaceae* | 27°F. |
|---|---|---|
| Yesterday, today and tomorrow | Spring-Summer | Brazil |

The common name is suggested by the fact that the two inch flowers open rich violet, fade to a blue-lavender and finally become white, so the three shades are always seen on this shrub at the same time. *Brunfelsia* grows to six feet with nearly evergreen glossy leaves. It is somewhat tender but grows equally well in coastal or inland areas. If in a very hot dry location, it appreciates part shade; it responds to rich, loose compost, liberal feeding during the growing season, and an adequate amount of water.

*Brunfelsia calycina macrantha* is slightly more spreading in form and has larger leaves and flowers to four inches across. *B. calycina eximia* has smaller leaves and blooms more profusely over a shorter period in spring. *B. americana*, with creamy fragrant flowers to four inches across, can be grown in the warmest gardens.

CALLIANDRA HAEMATOCEPHALA
*(C. inequilatera)*
Pink powder puff bush

| | |
|---|---|
| *Leguminosae* | 29°F. |
| Winter | Bolivia |

Somewhat tender, evergreen, probably at its best in the milder coastal areas, this aristocratic shrub also performs well in some inland areas, if given protection against a south or west wall. It bears large rose-pink, powder puff-like flower balls with showy colored stamens from fall to about March. It can be grown as a rounded shrub, six to eight feet tall, allowed to tumble over a wall, or espaliered against a wall, for which it is admirably suited. There is also a beautiful white variety.

CALLIANDRA TWEEDII
Trinidad flame bush

| | |
|---|---|
| *Leguminosae* | 25°F. |
| Spring and Fall | Brazil |

Trinidad flame bush is somewhat hardier than *C. haematocephala*. Its small, green, fern-like leaves make a pleasing contrast to the brilliant clusters of crimson stamens. It seldom grows higher than eight feet with an equal spread, and makes a colorful accent in southern California gardens either near the coast or in inland areas. It is fairly drought resistant but grows well under ordinary garden conditions provided it has very good drainage.

CARISSA MACROCARPA *(C. grandiflora)* *Apocynaceae* 26°F.
Natal plum Spring through Fall South Africa

This handsome evergreen shrub is noteworthy both for its one inch white flowers with orange blossom-like fragrance and its reddish small plum-like edible fruits, often appearing at the same time. The fruit can be eaten raw or cooked, the flavor resembling that of cranberries. All parts of the plant, including the fruit, contain a milky juice. The shrub grows to 18 feet and does equally well in coastal and inland areas. It is much branched and bears spines, making it a good hedge plant. Many cultivars are available, some dwarf compact plants with larger flowers, others lacking spines.

| CAMELLIA SASANQUA 'YULETIDE' | *Theaceae* | 15°F. |
|---|---|---|
| Sasanqua camellia | Fall-Winter | China, Japan |

Tidy appearance, profusion of colorful flowers during cool months and relative cold-hardiness explain the popularity of camellias in the subtropics. They are relatives of the tea plant, and legend has it that they came to England when shrewd Chinese merchants, to retain their monopoly on the tea trade, substituted camellias for tea plants when an English horticulturist tried to import live tea plants from China.

*Camellia sasanqua* is one of the three principal species seen among thousands of plants at Descanso Gardens in La Cañada, the others being *C. japonica* and *C. reticulata*. It is a graceful, small to medium-sized shrub with glossy evergreen leaves and three inch flowers in various shades of red, pink and white. Unlike most species, *C. sasanqua* does well even in almost full sun.

*C. japonica* is the most commonly available species. *C. reticulata* has the largest and showiest flowers though foliage is more sparse and the leggy stems call for lower shrubs such as azaleas or other camellias to be grown in front of them. Hybrids of this species with *C. japonica* combine the fine garden qualities of both species and doubtless many cultivars of this type will continue to be introduced. Because of the many cultivars available, varying in flower form and color, selections should be made from flowering plants.

Intriguing new *C.* X *williamsii* hybrids have come rapidly to prominence because of their adaptability to both sun and cold. These are crosses of *C. saluenensis* and *C. japonica*. One of the first of these, and still among the best, is *C.* X *williamsii* 'J.C. Williams.'

The foliage of camellias varies considerably but often is so handsome in floral arrangements that it is harvested for florist use. Pruning and disbudding will increase the quality of flowers, and sometimes the plants are treated with gibberellin to further increase flower size. A few have a delicate spicy fragrance and breeders are working to increase this characteristic. Camellias appreciate good drainage, slightly acid soil, should not be allowed to dry out and are intolerant of soil or mulch accumulating about the base of the trunk. Occasional applications of soil sulfur will be helpful to maintain soil acidity. Also acid residue fertilizers should be preferred.

| CHAMAELAUCIUM UNCINATUM | *Myrtaceae* | 27°F. |
| --- | --- | --- |
| Geraldton waxflower | Winter-Spring | Western Australia |

Useful both in the garden and for cut flowers, this six foot shrub with fine foliage and delicate sprays of flowers in varying shades of pink is one of the finest contributions of Australia to our local landscape and cut sprays are used by commercial florists. The plant blooms for at least three months and is benefitted by heavy pruning after flowering. It should be cut back approximately one-third of its height each year for maximum bloom. It needs good drainage, does not tolerate manure, and is equally happy near the coast or inland.

| CISTUS 'DORIS HIBBERSON' | *Cistaceae* | 20°F. |
|---|---|---|
| Rockrose | Spring | Mediterranean |

The discovery that these colorful, tough, hardy, evergreen, low-growing shrubs from the Mediterranean area are also fire-resistant has focused attention upon them during the past few years. The Los Angeles Arboretum, after conducting numerous experiments, has concluded that these plants may char when exposed to intense heat but do not burst into flame and has suggested their suitability for planting along firebreaks and in foothill areas. This and other *Cistus* species are quite drought tolerant, and mature plants should be watered with care to avoid root-rot.

The plant illustrated has three inch flowers. Other species have flowers which are white, lilac, or purple.

FUCHSIA 'SWINGTIME' | *Onagraceae* | 28°F.
Fuchsia | Summer and Other Seasons | Mexico, So. America

Especially adapted to the milder, moister coastal areas of the subtropics, the nearly 100 species of fuchsia are all native from Mexico to southern South America except for two found in New Zealand. The many named cultivars delight the eye with their crisp, jewel-like blossoms in various combinations of red, pink, purple, pastels and pure white, both single and double in form. The latter are often large, spectacular, and by far the most popular, though the singles have graceful flowers, abundant blossoms and greater resistance to sun and heat. They bloom mostly in the warmer months but in favored locations, with suitable pruning, will produce considerable winter bloom.

*F.* 'Swingtime,' which is illustrated, may grow to a height of six to eight feet with an equal spread. These growth characteristics make it adaptable for training as a formal tree, growing on a trellis, or using for a hanging basket as it is in the illustration.

Cultural requirements include well-drained soil rich in humus, partial shade, adequate watering, regular feeding with a complete fertilizer and correct pruning. Mulching is beneficial but the ground around fuchsias should not be penetrated with cultivating. Removal of spent flowers and fruits will help prolong the bloom period. Fuchsias are particularly effective for landscaping when several plants of one cultivar are massed together. They are not candidates for desert areas unless in a lath house equipped with a misting system.

GREYIA SUTHERLANDII | *Greyiaceae* Spring | 25°F. South Africa

The round, heart-shaped leaves and erect flower clusters of the greyias make them distinct from other plants. During most of the year, their foliage is attractive but at flowering time they are partially deciduous, revealing their stems. *G. sutherlandii* is by far the most attractive species. It becomes a woody shrub or small tree 10 to 15 feet high with scarlet flowers, characterized by prominent yellow stamens, arranged in dense clusters four to five inches long and broad. It grows natively to 6000 feet elevation, and therefore can withstand a reasonable amount of frost. Sometimes after warm winters the old brown leaves persist and have to be removed. *G. radlkoferi* is similar but has velvety leaves covered with soft whitish hairs.

| HIBISCUS HUEGELII | *Malvaceae* | 27°F. |
|---|---|---|
| Blue hibiscus | All Seasons | Australia |

The blue hibiscus, upper left, adds a delightful lilac-blue which is lacking in the color spectrum of the tropical *Hibiscus*. It is smaller, five feet tall, requires less water and tolerates slightly lower temperatures. The propeller-like flowers are four to five inches across and the leaves are rough and deeply divided. Individual flowers remain open on the plant for two or three days instead of a single day as in *H. rosa-sinensis*. It blooms at intervals throughout the year and requires occasional pruning to keep it from becoming 'leggy.'

*H. syriacus* or rose of sharon is a very hardy deciduous species from east Asia, available in a variety of colors. *H. pedunculatus*, from South Africa, is three or four feet high, evergreen, with small pinkish-mauve flowers like half-open trumpets, blooming during summer and fall and hardy to 25°F.

*H. schizopetalus*, with pendent red flowers with deeply cut petals and long-extended red columns of stamens, is a graceful shrub for the warmest areas.

*Hibiscus rosa-sinensis*, native of Asia and shown upper right, is the type seen in such splendor and variety in tropical countries though it is a marginal shrub for the subtropics. Some cultivars are hardier than others and a great deal of research is being done to develop new ones to increase the color combinations and cold tolerance. Most cultivars are evergreen shrubs about eight feet high. Their single or double flowers about six inches across come in a variety of colors and appear at intervals all year. The cultivar illustrated is 'Agnes Gault.'

Among the some 300 species are *H. elatus* from the West Indies, yellow or orange-red flowers; and *H. tiliaceus*, the Hawaiian tree hibiscus, which also has yellow blossoms fading to orange-red. Both are tree forms to 20 feet and bloom in summer.

HYPERICUM FLORIBUNDUM | *Hypericaceae* | 26°F.
St. John's wort | Summer | Canary and Madeira Islands

Golden one and a half to two inch flowers cover this six foot shrub during summer. Originating in the Mediterranean region it is ideally suited to southern California and thrives in most locations. There are many other species of shrub hypericums ranging in size to 15 feet, but averaging three to five feet. Most of them are evergreen and have yellow flowers.

*Hypericum calycinum, H. patulum henryi,* and the hybrid *H.* X *moserianum,* all attractive subshrubs one to three feet high with golden yellow flowers to three inches across, are hardy to 10°F. *H. coris* is a pretty one foot plant useful for a ground cover but cannot withstand severe frosts. *H.* 'Rowallane' is a handsome six foot shrub with three inch golden flowers.

JACOBINIA CARNEA | *Acanthaceae* | 28°F.
--- | --- | ---
 | Summer | Brazil

*Jacobinia carnea,* a sub-shrub with seven inch purplish leaves and eight inch heads of densely packed flowers at the end of every stem, is a handsome, exotic addition to any shade garden where frost is not severe. In colder areas it can be grown under glass or lath and set out in late spring for color to follow camellias and azaleas.

After flowering, the stems should be cut back to two or three nodes from the ground to keep the plant bushy and to renew blooming. Cuttings root easily and with judicious pinching, can be grown on to bloom as 18 to 24 inch pot or bedding plants.

*Jacobinia pauciflora floribunda* makes a pretty three foot shrub covered in winter with drooping red flowers tipped with yellow. It is tender to frost and does best in partial shade.

Several additional jacobinias are *J. radlkoferi,* similar to *J. carnea* but with velvety leaves; *J. aurea,* a shrub to 10 feet with striking, upright, terminal yellow inflorescences to 12 inches long; smaller *J. coccinea* with scarlet flowers in upright terminal heads; *J. ghiesbreghtiana,* a less tropical-looking shrub from Mexico, with scarlet or crimson flowers in loose panicles; and *J. incana,* with rust-red flowers, a somewhat hardier, gray-leaved, two foot sprawling shrub, making it a showy summer ground cover or basket plant.

| LEONOTIS LEONURUS | *Labiatae* | 20°F. |
|---|---|---|
| Lion's tail | Summer and Fall | South Africa |

This member of the sage family has a short, woody base, sending up shoots to a height of about six feet which in late summer and fall bear whorls of orange-yellow tubular flowers, surrounding the stem, successive tiers of flowers developing as it grows. After blooming, the flower-bearing stems should be pruned heavily. The flowers will keep in water for about three days if the cut stems are burned and then placed in water which has just boiled. The plants are not particular as to location, but heavy winds will break the soft flowering wood.

*L. nepetaefolia* from tropical Africa has broad, almost heart-shaped leaves and the flowers are not as neat and compact. *L. laxifolia* has broad-ovate leaves distinguishing it from the lance-shaped leaves of *L. leonurus.*

LEPTOSPERMUM SCOPARIUM — *Myrtaceae* — 25°F.

Tea tree — Winter-Spring — Australia-New Zealand

There are many cultivars of *L. scoparium* available in nurseries. The illustration is that of *L. scoparium* 'Red Damask,' one of the cultivars originating in California and growing at the Los Angeles Arboretum. It grows to about six feet, is evergreen with bronze-tinted foliage and has double, almost cerise-red flowers during winter and spring. 'Snow White' has masses of pure white flowers.

*L. scoparium* 'Nanum' is a dwarf form with pink flowers. *L. scoparium* 'Keatleyi' has large one inch pink flowers during winter and spring. *L. squarrosum*, an Australian species, grows to about eight feet with three-quarter inch, pink apple-blossom-like flowers in late summer and fall. *L. laevigatum* is tree-like to 20 feet, with single white flowers in spring and summer, shaggy bark and a bizarre twisted form. The tea trees do best in slightly acid sandy or gravelly soil.

| MAHONIA LOMARIIFOLIA | *Berberidaceae* | 25°F. |
| --- | --- | --- |
| Chinese hollygrape | Winter-Spring | China |

Probably the most decorative of the genus, *Mahonia lomariifolia* is an evergreen shrub branching close to the ground with multiple upright, thin woody stems to 12 feet, bearing 12 inch leaves divided into spiny leaflets. During winter the top of each branch is surmounted by an elongated cluster of small bright yellow flowers followed by blue berries.

Another useful species of *Mahonia* for subtropical climates is *M. bealei*, six to ten feet with large compound leaves and large plumes of fragrant yellow flowers in the spring. See page 174 for additional plants sometimes called mahonias.

| MONTANOA ARBORESCENS | *Compositae* | 27°F. |
|---|---|---|
| Daisy tree | Winter | Mexico |

The specimen in the photograph, growing in La Cañada, has successfully withstood a temperature of 27°F. with snow. It is over 15 years old and 12 feet tall, with a tree-like form but branching from the base. Evergreen, it blooms during the winter, reaching its climax about Christmas, when it is covered with white, daisy-like flowers with yellow centers. The striking effect of a shrubby tree covered with daisies at Christmas almost tempts one to rename it "White Christmas."

*Montanoa bipinnatifida* is more shrub-like, growing to about eight feet with deeply indented leaves and clusters of ball-shaped yellow and white double daisies. It blooms in late fall and early winter. *M. grandiflora* is a large shrub with upright shoots bearing three inch single daisy flowers. It also blooms in fall and winter. After blooming, both species should be pruned back heavily, but only the dead blossoms need to be cut in the case of *M. arborescens*. The Ruby Crowned Kinglet finds the dried seeds of *M. arborescens* a delectable feast.

| NERIUM OLEANDER | *Apocynaceae* | 20°F. |
|---|---|---|
| Oleander | Summer | Mediterranean |

Native to the Mediterranean region, oleanders have for many years been popular in California because of their hardiness, adaptability, summer-long colorful blossoms, and evergreen foliage. They are able to accommodate themselves to relatively dry conditions, and are much used along freeways, but they also grow and bloom profusely in areas of fairly heavy rainfall, such as Bermuda. A little extra water pays dividends in better flowering.

Oleanders are normally shrubs up to 15 feet, useful as specimen plants or hedges. They can be trained as trees, but continual maintenance is required to keep the new shoots pruned from the base. The white form makes a successful small tree. Different varieties make pleasing contrasts with their clusters of single or double, two to three inch flowers, in pink, red, salmon, yellowish and white.

| PROTEA | *Proteaceae* | 10°F. |
|---|---|---|
| | Winter-Spring | South Africa |

The large family Proteaceae is found primarily in the southern hemisphere, chiefly in South Africa with *Protea, Leucospermum, Leucadendron* and *Serruria,* and in Australia with *Grevillea, Hakea, Banksia, Telopea* and *Stenocarpus.* The great diversity in the genus *Protea* led early explorers to name it for the Greek god Proteus, who changed shape at will.

In southern California, members of the Protea family thrive near the coast. Large plantations of them are found near Escondido including many species of *Protea, Leucospermum, Leucadendron, Serruria, Paranomus* and *Telopea* and numerous *Banksia.* These plants must have good drainage, full sun and good air circulation; they do not like heavy fertilizing, excess alkalinity, or too much summer water. They tolerate cold to the mid-twenties.

*Protea suzannae* (lower photo opposite) is said to be the easiest to grow. *Leucospermum reflexum* (upper photo opposite) withstood a freeze of 27°F. and two inches of snow in La Cañada where it blooms for three months beginning in February. It has also been grown successfully in western Los Angeles.

*Grevillea banksii* (upper right) is a six to eight foot evergreen shrub from Australia. Other shrub grevilleas include *G. leucopteris* (white), *G. petrophiloides* (red and green), *G. thelemanniana* (red and yellow), *G. aquifolium* (red), *G. chrysodendron* (gold), *G.* 'Noel' (reddish), *G.* 'Constance' (orange), and *G. juniperina* 'Rosea' (rose). The grevilleas are valued as much for their handsome foliage as for their flowers.

*Banksia* is a remarkable genus of shrubs and trees from Australia, ranging from four to forty feet with brush-like flowers in various sizes, shapes and colors and saw-edged leaves. The cut flowers last 10 to 12 days and excite admiration. *B. occidentalis* (upper left) and *B. media* have almost identical golden honey-colored flowers and bloom from October until March.

OCHNA ATROPURPUREA | *Ochnaceae* | 27°F.
Mickey Mouse plant | Spring-Summer | South Africa

It is difficult for the uninitiated to realize that the above pictures are of the same plant, taken about three months apart. This beautiful and versatile shrub was formerly known in California as *Ochna multiflora*. There are about 85 species of *Ochna* including several trees such as *O. arborea* and *O. pulchra* which would be welcome additions to the landscape, but *O. atropurpurea* is presently the only species available in California. It grows moderately slowly, attaining a height of six feet in full sun or part shade, and espaliers well. The shrub is nearly evergreen though it thins out in late winter. In spring new leaves are followed by masses of bright yellow flowers resembling buttercups. After about eight weeks, the petals fall and the sepals and receptacle enlarge and turn scarlet, revealing four or five shiny black fruits. The name Mickey Mouse plant results from the often comic face appearance of the fruits. The color display spans a period of about five months. Mockingbirds find the ripe seeds irresistible so every year a few new ochnas spring up here and there to make fine candidates for transplanting to tubs, for gifts, hedge plants or for topiary treatment.

| PITTOSPORUM NAPAULENSE | *Pittosporaceae* | 25°F. |
|---|---|---|
| Golden fragrance | Spring | Himalayas |

The specimen in the photograph is growing at the Los Angeles Arboretum and was propagated from a parent specimen obtained a number of years ago from the U.S. Department of Agriculture and planted in what is now the Lux Arboretum, in the foothills above Monrovia, a facility of the Los Angeles Department of Arboreta and Botanic Gardens. It has been grown in southern California under the name of *Pittosporum floribundum.*

The shrub is a vigorous grower, attaining a height of 12 feet or more with a spread of at least eight feet. It has large glossy evergreen leaves and in the spring puts forth masses of intensely fragrant small golden-yellow flowers in terminal clusters.

Most of the familiar pittosporums are from Australia or Asia, and have white flowers. *P. tobira* grows to 10 feet, makes a good hedge, and also is available in a form with variegated leaves. *P. undulatum* is often grown as a shrub, but it tends to be tree-like and may reach 40 feet. Other tree pittosporums, such as *P. rhombifolium* and the weeping *P. phillyraeoides* have ornamental flowers and fruits.

| PUNICA GRANATUM 'LEGRELLEAE' | *Punicaceae* | 10°F. |
|---|---|---|
| Double-flowered pomegranate | Summer | Europe, Asia |

The specimen illustrated is a variegated form of the double-flowered pomegranate, a large deciduous shrub or shrubby tree to 15 feet. The commonest form of this species has large three inch bright orange-red flowers, blooming throughout the summer months. In the variegated form occasional flowers revert to the original orange-red, as shown in the photograph. There is a dwarf form known as *P. granatum* 'Nana' which is only a few feet high, has small flowers and miniature fruits.

*Punica granatum* 'Florepleno' is a double-flowering pomegranate from southern Europe which grows to a 20 foot small tree, has bright orange-red flowers, produces no fruit, and is hardy.

The single-flowered fruiting plant *P. granatum* appears in writings of antiquity and is believed to have been introduced into southern Europe by the Carthaginians. The dark red apple-sized fruits are divided into tiny compartments containing seeds and a red cranberry-flavored juice. When ripe, fruits pop open on the trees and are enjoyed by various birds.

| PYRACANTHA COCCINEA | *Rosaceae* | 10°F. |
| --- | --- | --- |
| Firethorn | Fall-Winter | So. Europe-W. Asia |

This hardy, large, evergreen, thorny member of the rose family, one of a number of species and cultivars of *Pyracantha,* is covered in the spring with masses of small white flowers. During the fall and early winter these are replaced by bright red fruits in large clusters which almost hide the leaves and are so brilliant and conspicuous as to thoroughly justify the name "Firethorn."

The fruits vary in color from orange to scarlet, depending upon the variety, and continue for two or three months. As they become ripe and mellow, they are regarded as delicious little apples, especially by mocking birds, robins and cedar waxwings. Let the birds enjoy these berries; they are eaten only when fully ripe and ready to fall anyway.

Pyracanthas are occasionally attacked by fire blight, causing branches, foliage and fruit, to turn brown. Since fire blight is a bacterial infection, the affected branch should be destroyed, and the pruning shears sterilized.

| | | |
|---|---|---|
| RHAPHIOLEPIS INDICA 'SPRINGTIME' | *Rosaceae* | 15°F. |
| Indian hawthorn | Spring | So. China |

Although its name suggests an origin in India, this thornless, evergreen, five foot shrub is a native of southern China. It has handsome, leathery, shiny three inch leaves and conspicuous masses of half-inch flowers. The flowers are followed by small purplish-black fruits. Improved cultivars, with white, pink, and red flowers and a variety of habits, are available.

This hardy evergreen is one of our finest shrubs for landscape use over a wide area in southern California. Not only is it a good foundation plant, but the flowers, especially the pinks, are excellent for cutting. Best blooming period is at Easter time.

## RONDELETIA CORDATA
Heartleaf rondeletia

| *Rubiaceae* | 30°F. |
|---|---|
| Spring-Summer | Guatemala |

This attractive but tender shrub is suitable only for relatively frost-free areas, especially near the coast. It belongs in a tropical family that includes *Coffea*, *Cinchona* (quinine tree), *Gardenia* and *Bouvardia*. It is being grown successfully in Bel-Air and other parts of western Los Angeles. The photograph was taken on the UCLA Campus.

The shrub is evergreen, grows to about seven feet and blooms in spring and summer, with clusters of small, tubular, pink to red flowers with yellow throats.

Another species, *R. amoena* from Central America, which is slightly less showy but still attractive, is being grown here in milder areas.

## SOLANUM RANTONNETII

| Paraguay nightshade | *Solanaceae* | 20°F. |
|---|---|---|
| | Spring-Fall | Argentina |

The attractive evergreen semi-vining shrub with its masses of blue-violet, fragrant flowers affords an enticing background to the old-fashioned gate lantern shown in the photograph on page 57. One would scarcely realize that it is a relative of the weed known as deadly nightshade, or, for that matter, of the potato, tomato, or petunia. It grows to seven feet or more, with clusters of one inch flowers from spring to fall. It seems equally happy in coastal or inland regions, is drought resistant, but will tolerate average lawn conditions. It is said to provide a maximum display of flowers when given heavy feeding and generous watering, yet the specimen in the photograph was apparently growing under very dry conditions. It can be trained to a single standard, making a miniature tree.

| STREPTOSOLEN JAMESONII | *Solanaceae* | 30°F. |
| --- | --- | --- |
| Marmalade bush | Spring-Summer | Peru to Colombia |

The casual observer would scarcely recognize the relationship of this gaudy, yellow to orange-red-flowered shrub to the quiet, dignified, purple *Solanum rantonnetii* depicted on page 57 and described on page 85. *Streptosolen jamesonii* is evergreen, reaches six feet, with loose, twisty branches, and blooms for several months during spring and summer. The showy flowers are in terminal clusters, the petals forming a spirally twisted tube at the base which widens out at the top. Somewhat frost-tender, this plant is best suited to milder, coastal areas. It needs sun and fast drainage.

| TECOMA STANS | *Bignoniaceae* | 27°F. |
|---|---|---|
| Yellow elder | Fall | Florida, Arizona<br>Mexico, So. America |

This erect shrub, growing to six feet, is considered one of the finest ornamental shrubs native to the United States. It is evergreen and blooms during the fall with clusters of yellow trumpet-shaped flowers about one and a half inches long. It grows inland but is probably a little more lush and showy near the coast. It performs especially well in the San Diego area. The specimen in the photograph is growing at Palm Desert. In colder inland areas, if it is frozen back, it may bloom again the following year from new wood springing from the base. In warm areas it may become a small tree.

## TIBOUCHINA URVILLEANA

Princess flower

| *Melastomataceae* | 27°F. |
|---|---|
| Summer-Fall-Winter | Brazil |

The rich royal purple of the two to three inch velvety flowers amply justifies the name "princess flower" for this handsome six to ten foot Brazilian shrub with its rich evergreen silky-hairy leaves. It flowers several months during summer, fall and winter, depending upon location. It may be grown in full sun near the coast, but in hotter, drier inland areas it appreciates part shade. Good drainage and a slightly acid soil are important.

*T. holosericea* has slightly smaller purple flowers and more silky leaves. *T. mutabilis* has flowers which change from deep rose to white. *T. granulosa* is a small tree with either purple or pink flowers.

## VIBURNUM MACROCEPHALUM

Chinese snowball

| *Caprifoliaceae* | 5°F. |
|---|---|
| Spring-Summer | China |

The Chinese snowball, largest of the viburnums, grows to ten feet or more and presents a stunning sight when covered with its globose flower-heads each some five inches in diameter, at first light chartreuse in color, maturing to pure white. The Chinese snowball has much larger clusters than the common snowball, *V. opulus*, and is not completely deciduous in winter and less plagued by aphids in summer. Many other deciduous and evergreen viburnums are available.

ADDITIONAL FLOWERING SHRUBS OF MERIT

This list includes vining or sprawling shrubs which can be trained on a wall or allowed to droop over a bank, designated here as VS. Small shrubs which may have partially herbaceous stems are designated SS. WGB indicates Sunset Western Garden Book.

| | Species | Family | Common Name | Origin | Height to | Color | Season of Color | Hardy to | Placement |
|---|---|---|---|---|---|---|---|---|---|
| | Abelia X grandiflora | Caprifoliaceae | glossy abelia | garden | 8′ | pink & white | July-October | Hardy | Sun or part shade |
| | A. X g. 'Prostrata' & A. X g. 'Sherwoodii' | —more appropriate for the small garden | | | 3′ | pink & white | July-October | Hardy | Sun or part shade |
| | Abutilon hybridum | Malvaceae | flowering maple | garden | 10′ | white, pink, red, yellow, apricot | all year | 25°F. | Part shade |
| | Acokanthera oblongifolia *(A. spectabilis)* | Apocynaceae | bushman's poison | Africa | 10′ | pink & white | all year (esp. spring) | 25°F. | Sun or light shade |
| | Alberta magna | Rubiaceae | | So. Africa | 15′ | scarlet | winter-spring | Light frost | Sun |
| | Alyogyne hakeaefolia | Malvaceae | | Australia | 6′ | lilac-blue | spring-summer | Hardy | Sun |
| | Berberis darwinii | Berberidaceae | | Chile | 10′ | orange, yellow | spring | Hardy | Sun or part shade |
| | **B. X stenophylla** | | | garden | 6′ | golden yellow | spring | Hardy | Sun |
| SS | Bouvardia leiantha 'Fire Chief' | Rubiaceae | | garden | 3′ | coral-rose | spring-fall | Light frost | Sun or part shade |
| SS | B. longiflora 'Albatross' | | | garden | 3′ | white | spring-fall | Light frost | Sun or part shade |
| | Buddleia asiatica | Loganiaceae | white butterfly bush | China-India | 3′ | white | winter-spring | Tender | Sun & good drainage |
| | Burchellia bubalina | Rubiaceae | wild pomegranate | So. Africa | 10′ | coral red | summer | Light frost | Shade |
| VS | Candollea cuneiformis | Dilleniaceae | | Australia | 6′ | yellow | spring | Light frost | Sun & good drainage |
| VS | Cantua buxifolia | Polemoniaceae | flower of Incas | Andes | 5′ | cerise | spring-summer | 27°F. | Light shade |
| SS | Caryopteris incana | Verbenaceae | blue spiraea | China, Japan | 3′ | lavender-blue | summer-fall | Light frost | Sun, light soil |
| SS | C. X clandonensis 'Heavenly Blue' | | blue mist | garden | 2′ | deep blue | fall | Hardy | Sun |
| | Cestrum aurantiacum | Solanaceae | orange cestrum | C. America | 8′ | orange | late spring-summer | 25°F. | Sun or part shade |
| | C. diurnum | | day jessamine | West Indies | 15′ | white | summer | 25°F. | Sun or part shade |

| | Species | Family | Common Name | Origin | Height to | Color | Season of Color | Hardy to | Placement |
|---|---|---|---|---|---|---|---|---|---|
| | **Cestrum fasciculatum 'Newellii'** | | red cestrum | | 10′ | crimson or scarlet | spring-summer | 25°F. | Sun or part shade |
| | C. purpureum *(C. elegans)* (var. smithii is pink) | | | Mexico | 10′ | rosy red | all year | 25°F. | Sun or part shade |
| | Choisya ternata | Rutaceae | Mexican orange | Mexico | 8′ | white | spring | 15°F. | Sun or part shade |
| SS | Chorizema cordatum | Leguminosae | flame pea | Australia | 5′ | orange & red | spring-summer | Light frost | Sun or part shade |
| SS | C. ilicifolium and C. varium | | | Australia | 2′-3′ | orange & red | spring-summer | Light frost | Sun or part shade |
| | Clerodendrum fragrans | Verbenaceae | Glory bower | China, Japan | 8′ | white, pink | summer | Light frost | Sun or part shade |
| | C. ugandense | | blue clerodendron | Uganda | 10′ | blue | August | 25°F. | Sun or part shade |
| SS | Clianthus formosus | Leguminosae | glory pea | Australia | 4′ | scarlet | summer | Light frost | Hot, dry bank |
| | Coleonema album | Rutaceae | breath of heaven | So. Africa | 5′ | white | September-April | 24°F. | Sun & fast drainage |
| | C. pulchrum | | pink breath of heaven | So. Africa | 5′ | pink | September-April | 24°F. | Sun & fast drainage |
| | Corokia cotoneaster | Cornaceae | | New Zealand | 10′ | yellow | spring | 10°F. | Sun or part shade |
| | Correa alba | Rutaceae | Australian fuchsia | Australia | 4′ | white | summer | 20°F. | Sun or part shade |
| | C. backhousiana, 5′ with chartreuse flowers; C. X harrisii, 2½′, clear red; and C. pulchella, 2½′, pink flowers are winter flowering | | | | | | | | |
| | Crotalaria agatiflora | Leguminosae | canary bird bush | Africa | 12′ | chartreuse | summer-fall | 28°F. | Sun or part shade |
| SS | Cuphea hyssopifolia | Lythraceae | false heather | Mexico | 2′ | white, pink or purple | summer | 25°F. | Sun or part shade |
| SS | C. ignea | | cigar plant | Mexico | 1′ | red | summer-fall | 25°F. | Sun or part shade |
| SS | C. micropetala | | | Mexico | 2′ | yellow & red | summer-fall | 25°F. | Sun or part shade |
| | Cytisus canariensis | Leguminosae | canary broom | Canaries | 6′ | yellow | spring-summer | 15°F. | Sun, fast drainage |
| | C. scoparius | | scotch broom | Europe | 10′ | yellow | spring-summer | Hardy | Sun |
| | 'Ruby Glow' | | | garden | 1′ | rose-pink | spring-fall | Hardy | Part shade |
| | Daphne caucasica | Thymelaeaceae | deciduous daphne | Caucasus | 3′ | pinkish-white | all summer | Hardy | Part shade |
| | D. cneorum 'Ruby Glow' | | garland daphne | garden | 1′ | rose-pink | spring-fall | Hardy | Part shade |

| | Species | Family | Common Name | Origin | Height to | Color | Season of Color | Hardy to | Placement |
|---|---|---|---|---|---|---|---|---|---|
| | Daphne odora 'Rose Queen' (deciduous) | | winter daphne | garden | 4' | pink | Feb. Mar. | Hardy | Part shade |
| | | Thymelaeaceae | | Caucasus | 3' | pinkish white | all summer | Hardy | Part shade |
| | Datura candida | Solanaceae | angel's trumpet | Peru | 15' | white | summer-fall | Light frost | Sun |
| | D. sanguinea | | | Peru | 15' | orange, red | summer | 32°F. | Sun |
| | D. suaveolens | | angel's trumpet | Brazil | 15' | white | summer | Light frost | Sun |
| | Deutzia pulchra | Saxifragaceae | evergreen deutzia | Philippines | 10' | white | spring | Hardy | Sun or part shade |
| SS | Diosma ericoides | Rutaceae | breath of heaven | So. Africa | 2' | white | winter, spring | 24°F. | Sun |
| | Dodonaea viscosa 'Purpurea' | Sapindaceae | purple hop bush | West Indies | 15' | purple foliage | winter | 24°F. | Sun |
| | Duranta erecta grandiflora | Verbenaceae | sky flower | Trop. America | 15' | blue flowers, golden berries | most of year | 25°F. | Sun |
| SS | Eranthemum nervosum | Acanthaceae | | Tropical Asia | 4' | blue | spring | 32°F. | Sun or part shade |
| | Erica carnea and its cultivars | Ericaceae | | European Alps | 6'-18' | white, pink, red | December-June | Hardy | Shade, acid soil |
| | E. mammosa 'Jubilee' | | | So. Africa | 3' | salmon pink | spring, repeating | 25°F. | Shade |
| | E. vagans 'Lyonesse' 18", white; and E. v. 'Mrs. D. F. Maxwell' cherry pink or red | | | | | | July-October | Hardy | Shade |
| | Escallonia spp. & cvs. | Saxifragaceae | | So. America | 25' | white to red | most of year | 20°F. | Sun or part shade |
| SS | Eupatorium sordidum | Compositae | mist flower | Mexico | 5' | violet blue | summer | 20°F. | Sun or part shade |
| SS | Euphorbia milii *(E. splendens)* | Euphorbiaceae | crown of thorns | Madagascar | 4' | pink, red, yellow & orange | all | Light frost | Part shade |
| | E. pulcherrima Ecke cvs. | | poinsettia | Mexico | 8' | red, pink, white | winter | 25°F. | Sun |
| | Euryops athanasiae | Compositae | So. African tree daisy | So. Africa | 6' | yellow | winter | Light frost | Sun & good drainage |
| | E. pectinatus | | golden shrub daisy | So. Africa | 3' | yellow | all year | Light frost | Sun & good drainage |
| | Exochorda X macrantha 'The Bride' | Rosaceae | | garden | 4' | white | late April | Hardy | Sun |
| | E. racemosa | | pearl bush | China | 15' | white | April | Hardy | Sun |
| | Fabiana imbricata | Solanaceae | | Peru | 8' | white | several times a year | 25°F. | Sun |
| | Forsythia cultivars | Oleaceae | | Asia | 10' | yellow | winter-spr. | Hardy | Sun |

| | Species | Family | Common Name | Origin | Height to | Color | Season of Color | Hardy to | Placement |
|---|---|---|---|---|---|---|---|---|---|
| | Gardenia, spp. & cvs. | Rubiaceae | | China, Africa | 20′ | white | summer, winter | 25°F. | Shade |
| SS | Gnidia polystachya | Thymelaeaceae | | So. Africa | 6′ | pale yellow | spring | 30°F. | Sun |
| VS | Grewia caffra | Tiliaceae | lavender star plant | So. Africa | 10′ | lavender | late spring to fall | 24°F. | Sun |
| | Hakea cucullata | Proteaceae | | Australia | 14′ | pink | spring | Light frost | Sun & good drainage |
| | H. multilineata | | | Australia | 12′ | deep red | spring | Light frost | Sun & good drainage |
| SS | Halimium lasianthum | Cistaceae | | Portugal | 3′ | yellow | spring | 24°F. | Sun |
| | Hebe 'Autumn Glory' | Scrophulariaceae | | garden | 2′ | dark lavender-blue | late summer, fall | 15°F. | Sun or part shade |
| | H. 'Reevesii' ('Evansii') | | | garden | 3′ | reddish purple | summer | 25° F. | Sun or part shade |
| SS | Helianthemum nummularium cultivars | Cistaceae | sunroses | Mediterranean | 8″ x 3′ spread | yellow, peach, pink, red | April-June | Hardy | Sun & good drainage |
| SS | Heliotropium arborescens | Boraginaceae | cherry pie | Peru | 4′ | violet or purple | summer | Tender | Sun or part shade |
| SS | Helleborus argutifolius *(H. corsicus)* | Ranunculaceae | Corsican hellebore | Corsica | 3′ | pale green | late fall-late spring | Hardy | Shade or part shade |
| SS | H. niger | | Christmas rose | Europe | 18″ | white, turning purplish | December-April | Hardy | Shade or part shade |
| SS | H. orientalis | | lenten rose | Asia minor | 18″ | greenish or purplish | March-May | Hardy | Shade or part shade |
| VS | Holmskioldia sanguinea | Verbenaceae | Chinese hat | Himalayas | 15′ | rust | all year | 22°F. | Sun or part shade |
| | Hydrangea macrophylla | Saxifragaceae | lace cap hydrangea | China, Japan | 12′ | blue, pink | summer, fall | Hardy | Part shade |
| SS | Iboza riparia | Labiatae | misty plume bush | So. Africa | 6′ | lilac, purple | fall, winter | Light frost | Shade |
| VS | Iochroma cyaneum | Solanaceae | | Colombia | 8′ | blue or purple | summer, fall | Light frost | Sun or part shade |
| | I. coccineum | | | C. America | 8′ | scarlet | summer, fall | Light frost | Sun or part shade |
| | Justicia fulvicoma *(Beloperone guttata)* | Acanthaceae | shrimp plant | Mexico | 4′ | copper bracts | all year | Light frost | Sun or part shade |
| | Kerria japonica 'Pleniflora' | Rosaceae | | China | 8′ | yellow | March-May | Hardy | Part shade |
| | Lavandula dentata | Labiatae | French lavender | Mediterranean | 3′ | purple | spring, summer, fall | 24°F. | Sun & fast drainage |
| | Leucophyllum frutescens | Scrophulariaceae | Texas ranger | Texas, Mexico | 10′ | rosy purple | summer | 20°F. | For hot desert areas |

| | Species | Family | Common Name | Origin | Height to | Color | Season of Color | Hardy to | Placement |
|---|---|---|---|---|---|---|---|---|---|
| VS | Loropetalum chinense | Hamamelidaceae | | China | 6′ | whitish | March, April | 27°F. | Sun or part shade |
| | Luculia gratissima | Rubiaceae | | Himalayas | 8′ | pink or rose | fall-winter | 30°F. | Part shade |
| | Lygos *(Genista)* monosperma | Leguminosae | bridal veil broom | Mediterranean | 10′ | white | late winter-spring | 27°F. | Sun |
| | Mackaya bella | Acanthaceae | | So. Africa | 5′ | mauve | spring-summer | 27°F. | Shade or part shade |
| | Malvaviscus arboreus penduliflorus | Malvaceae | | Mexico | 15′ | red | summer-fall | 25°F. | Part shade or sun |
| | Murraya paniculata | Rutaceae | orange jessamine | India, Malaya | 12′ | white | summer-fall | 27°F. | Part shade |
| | Nandina domestica | Berberidaceae | heavenly bamboo | China, Japan | 8′ | pinkish fls. & red berries | spring-summer | Hardy | Sun or part shade |
| SS | Nierembergia scoparia *(N. frutescens)* | Solanaceae | cup flower | Chile | 3′ | white or violet | summer | 20°F. | Sun & good drainage |
| SS | Odontospermum sericeum | Compositae | | Canary Is. | 3′ | yellow | summer | 25°F. | Sun |
| | Paeonia suffruticosa | Ranunculaceae | tree peony | China | 6′ | rose, red, or white | spring | Hardy | Sun or part shade |
| SS | Pentas lanceolata | Rubiaceae | | Africa | 5′ | pink, red, white, lavender | almost all year | Light frost | Part shade |
| SS | Phlomis fruticosa | Labiatae | Jerusalem sage | So. Europe | 4′ | yellow | early summer | 24°F. | Sun, poor soil |
| | Photinia glabra | Rosaceae | Japanese photinia | Japan | 10′ | white | summer | Light frost | Sun |
| SS | Pimelia ferruginea | Thymelaeaceae | rosy rice flower | Australia | 3′ | rosy pink | early summer & intermittently | Light frost | Part shade |
| | Podalyria calyptrata | Leguminosae | sweetpea bush | So. Africa | 12′ | mauve, white | spring | Light frost | Sun |
| | Poinciana gilliesii | Leguminosae | bird of paradise | So. America | 10′ | yellow, red stamens | all summer | 27°F. | Sun & good drainage |
| | Polygala X dalmaisiana | Polygalaceae | **sweetpea shrub** | garden | 5′ | rosy red or purplish | all year | 24°F. | Sun or part shade |
| | P. virgata | | | So. Africa | 8′ | purple | fall-winter | Hardy | Sun & good drainage |
| SS | Potentilla fruticosa (deciduous) | Rosaceae | cinquefoil | China | 3′ | bright yellow | June-October—(See WGB for many named varieties) | | |
| | Prostanthera rotundifolia | Labiatae | mint bush | Australia | 6′ | lilac blue | April, May | Light frost | Sun or part shade |

| | Species | Family | Common Name | Origin | Height to | Color | Season of Color | Hardy to | Placement |
|---|---|---|---|---|---|---|---|---|---|
| SS | Reinwardtia indica | Linaceae | yellow flax | India | 4′ | yellow | fall-winter | 24°F. | Sun or part shade |
| | Rhigozum obovatum | Bignoniaceae | karroo gold | So. Africa | 8′ | yellow | summer | 24°F. | Sun |
| | Rosmarinus officinalis | Labiatae | rosemary | Europe | 3′ | lilac to purple | all year | Hardy | Sun |
| SS | Ruellia macrantha | Acanthaceae | | Brazil | 6′ | rosy purple | spring-summer | Tender | Part shade |
| SS | Ruspolia seticalyx | Acanthaceae | | Rhodesia | 2′ | salmon or red | summer | Light frost | Part shade |
| SS | Russelia equisetiformis | Scrophulariaceae | coral-bell bush | Mexico | 4′ | coral-red | all year | Light frost | Sun |
| | Salvia fulgens | Labiatae | cardinal salvia | Mexico | 3′ | scarlet | late spring-summer | Tender | Sun & good drainage |
| | S. greggii | | autumn sage | Mexico | 4′ | rosy red | fall | 25°F. | Sun |
| | S. leucantha | | Mexican bush sage | Mexico | 4′ | purple or rose | summer, fall | 25°F. | Sun |
| | Schotia speciosa (*S. afra*) | Leguminosae | Hottentot's bean | So. Africa | 10′ | bright red | spring | 30°F. | Sun |
| VS | Sollya fusiformis | Pittosporaceae | Australian bluebell | Australia | 3′ | blue | summer | 25°F. | Sun or part shade |
| | Sparmannia africana | Tiliaceae | African linden | So. Africa | 20′ | white | mid-winter | 30°F. | Sun |
| | Spartium junceum | Leguminosae | Spanish broom | Mediterranean | 10′ | yellow | spring, summer | 18°F. | Sun, poor soil |
| SS | Sutera grandiflora | Scrophulariaceae | wild phlox | So. Africa | 3′ | blue | all year | 25°F. | Sun or part shade |
| | Syringa (lilac), deciduous flowering shrubs—S. vulgaris 'Lavender Lady' & S. laciniata (persian lilac) are among those which can be grown in southern California | | | | | | | | |
| | Tamarix parviflora | Tamaricaceae | | Europe, Asia | 12′ | pink, white | spring | 20°F. | For hot desert areas |
| | Tecoma garrocha | Bignoniaceae | Argentine tecoma | Argentina | 10′ | coral or salmon with scarlet tube | summer | Light frost | Sun & heat |
| | Templetonia retusa | Leguminosae | cockies tongues | Australia | 6′ | brick-red | winter-spring | 25°F. | Sun or part shade |
| | Teucrium fruticans | Labiatae | germander | Europe | 4′ | blue | summer | Hardy | Sun |
| SS | Turraea obtusifolia | Meliaceae | star bush | So. Africa | 4′ | white | fall, & intermittent | 26°F. | Perfect drainage, part shade |
| | Vitex agnus-castus (deciduous) | Verbenaceae | chaste tree | So. Europe | 10′ | lilac blue | late summer-fall | 20°F. | Sun |
| | Weigelia cvs. | Caprifoliaceae | | East Asia | 10′ | yellow, pink, red | spring | Hardy | Sun or part shade |

# FLOWERING VINES

*see page 116*

# *Chapter III*

# FLOWERING VINES FOR YEAR-ROUND COLOR

This chapter contains some of the most colorful of the numerous vining ornamentals for enhancing fences and facades, hillsides and retaining walls. Vines can dramatize the most effectively designed architecture and soften less pleasing structures. They can cover chain link and drape and conceal concrete. Gardeners in subtropical climates have the advantage of being able to grow well more kinds of vining plants than those in other climatic zones.

Described in this chapter are but a few of the infinite possibilities. Purposely omitted are valuable vining materials having inconspicuous flowers such as the evergreen grapes, ivies, creeping fig, etc. It cannot be over-emphasized that chapter categories are somewhat arbitrary and many highly desirable colorful plants which are not true vines can be used successfully for a vining effect such as an espalier, but are more properly listed under shrubs and California native plants. Some examples of these are: *Solanum rantonnetii*, on pages 57 and 85; *Calliandra haematocephala*, page 62, and *Camellia sasanqua*, pages 64 and 65. Also the climbing aloes on page 162 should be noted.

Some vines (as well as some shrubs also) may be trained horizontally on the ground as ground covers, or down over cliffs or rocks as illustrated by *Bougainvillea*, pages 100, 101, 102.

When a plant of any kind is intended to clothe a wall or fence it is imperative that structural assistance be provided. Only a very few vines will attach themselves voluntarily and even these must be spread on the new surface and encouraged with some kind of attachment. If a trellis is used it should be sturdy, adequate and attached firmly to the wall surface. Never rely on flimsy inadequate trellises. The excess portions of the plant which do not spread effectively should be removed. Plant location and pruning recommendations are given when important. Additional vines of merit are listed on page 129.

| ACTINIDIA CHINENSIS | *Actinidiaceae* | 20°F. |
|---|---|---|
| Chinese gooseberry | Spring | China |

This handsome deciduous vine of burgeoning proportions produces striking two inch white flowers that age to pale yellow. The hairy thin-skinned edible fruits are pale brown, green inside. Strong thick stems twist and twine around any structure available, making a study in rhythm and line. The deciduous leaves are some five inches long, dark green, conspicuously ribbed and woolly silver on the undersides. Chinese gooseberry is seen frequently in central California but is occasionally grown in the south and probably could be used more. It likes some winter chilling, sun or partial shade, ample moisture, and needs strong support—heavy overhead structure is ideal. For satisfactory fruiting it is necessary to have two plants, a male and female, or a grafted plant possessing both sexes. Prune after fruit is picked. Fruit from New Zealand is offered in local markets as kiwi.

| ANTIGONON LEPTOPUS | *Polygonaceae* | 15°F. |
|---|---|---|
| Coral vine | Late Summer-Fall | Mexico |

Tumbling skeins of electric pink identify antigonon in the autumn, especially in the lower desert regions. The abundantly massed tiny flowers cover the golden-green massed foliage as the vine clambers unrestrainedly over fences, shrubbery, trees and roofs—even carpeting large patches of hot bare earth as in its native Mexico. Occasionally the blossoms are softer pink, sometimes white or neon crimson. A lover of heat and strong sun, the coral vine usually performs poorly in cool coastal gardens but is increasingly brilliant and vigorous as one travels inland where it dies to a rusty crown with frost. This means a clean-up job in the winter, though the roots survive briefly frozen ground and produce new growth with the return of warm weather.

| ARISTOLOCHIA ELEGANS | *Aristolochiaceae* | 28°F. |
|---|---|---|
| Calico flower | Summer | Brazil |

*Aristolochia* is a large genus of perennial plants, mostly climbers, not commonly cultivated in California. It usually has large heart-shaped leaves and flaring-tubed, strangely formed blossoms suggesting pipes or speckled abstract art objects. Various species occur in warm moist climates. There is one California native *(A. californica)* and at least one very hardy species *(A. durior)* native to eastern United States, both known as dutchman's pipe. The species illustrated *(A. elegans)* is occasionally grown here and blooms reasonably well in summer though it usually dies back in winter. It wants a warm-summer garden, ample moisture and good soil. Its rather unbelievable three-inch blossoms are white-veined, brownish-purple outside, purple-brown veined with yellow inside and edged with long hairs, certainly conversation pieces.

BOUGAINVILLEA | *Nyctaginaceae* | 32°F.
All Year | South America

No vine is more characteristic of southern California than bougainvillea. In this area many a house has been sold by its appealing bougainvillea spilling over roof or patio walls. In frost-free areas this semi-deciduous to evergreen vine should be planted in far greater numbers for its spectacular color which lasts most of the year.

Planting cultivars of different shades together can produce a scintillating color effect (see page 102). Flowers of bougainvillea are actually inconspicuous, the bright colors come from the bracts surrounding the tiny flowers. Colors range from magenta-purple through purplish pinks to crimson in *B. spectabilis (B. brasiliensis)* and in the cultivars 'Texas Dawn,' 'Rose Queen,' 'Barbara Karst,' 'San Diego Red,' *B.* X *buttiana* 'Mrs. Butt' ('Crimson Lake'), and 'Crimson Jewel.' Colors range from deep bronze through orange and gold to salmon in the cultivars 'Afterglow,' *B.* X *buttiana* 'Orange King,' 'California King,' 'California Gold,' and 'Mrs. Praetorius.' The selection *B. spectabilis* 'Lateritia' is truly brick red. Pure white are *B.* 'Madonna,' *B.* 'Convent,' and *B.* 'Jamaica White.' The whites are very tender with 'Jamaica White' the best of the three.

Bougainvilleas are vines for the hottest possible exposures. They grow and bloom best in soil that is neither rich nor constantly watered and where the sun hits the entire plant, including its root-run, without obstruction of any kind, even ground cover or mulch. Planting against a light-reflecting wall is ideal. Most cultivars are rampant growers and require plenty of space or else frequent pruning. A few cultivars, such as 'Temple Fire,' are compact and shrubby, making good ground covers, spilling over retaining walls, or scrambling on hot rocky banks. Minimum watering after the plant is established gives maximum flowering and minimum leaf growth.

All bougainvilleas are good for growing overhead on trellises, in trees having thin foliage, or on roofs or walls, inland or near the seacoast. Also they may be trained to form hedges or clipped for formal effects. Florists have used them as pot plants. They are trained to make small street trees in Brazil where they are native.

Most bougainvilleas should be planted in relatively frost-free areas; however, frost-damaged plants often grow back quickly after a severe freeze. They should not be pruned or planted during cold weather. Poor soil and reduced watering late in the year may help to ripen the wood and make them more resistant to frost. For colder areas, the old familiar purple *Bougainvillea spectabilis* is best as it can stand about ten degrees lower temperature than other species. The bush types such as 'Temple Fire' and 'Crimson Jewel' may be grown in large containers and moved under shelter during severe freezing periods.

The upper photo on page 102 is *B.* X *buttiana* 'Orange King.' In the lower picture, *B. spectabilis* is intertwined with an unusually red form of 'Mrs. Praetorius.' The third flowering plant in the lower picture on page 102 is *Lantana camara* (see page 149), a bright scrambling shrub. An additional bougainvillea in a rich blaze of color is shown on page 34 in front of a *Tipuana tipu* tree.

| ROSA BANKSIAE 'LUTEA' | *Rosaceae* | 15°F. |
| --- | --- | --- |
| Lady Banks' rose | Winter-Spring | China |

Evergreen and usually thornless, this old Chinese species climber is timeless and useful in California. Best known and loved is the double light yellow form 'Lutea' which may begin its long season in early winter and climax in March with clouds of faintly fragrant small flowers in generous clusters of softest pale gold, a color especially pleasant with other spring flowers. The leaves are small, sparse and shining, usually pestless and without mildew. Like most species roses it's an abundant grower capable of 20 feet, but it tolerates drastic pruning when blossoms are gone and this often results in another lesser wave of bloom. It likes sun or partial shade and much moisture. If pruned in winter, flowering wood will be removed. The species has fragrant white double flowers.

Another handsome climbing rose is 'Mermaid' which has single pale yellow flowers and a vigorous growth habit.

BAUHINIA GALPINII | *Leguminosae* | 28°F.
Summer-Fall | South Africa

This bauhinia, an excitingly showy vining shrub, is ideal for a long south-facing fence, as is the blue plumbago pictured with it on the opposite page and described below. It needs fast drainage, a warm root-run, and a frost-free location. Although slow to start it will attain a 20 foot spread. Its open structure, little, light green kidney-shaped leaves and generous clusters of one and one-half inch salmon to orange-red flowers which appear in late summer and autumn make it a most desirable garden subject. Any necessary pruning should be done immediately after blooms fade.

*Bauhinia corymbosa*, a native of eastern Asia, is a climbing species with pink flowers.

PLUMBAGO AURICULATA | *Plumbaginaceae* | 25°F.
*(P. capensis)*
Plumbago | Summer-Fall | South Africa

The clear light blue masses of phlox-like flowers of plumbago may be seen along freeways and in some of southern California's older gardens. Occasionally plumbago is pure white. From spring to late fall this vining shrub romps freely, sometimes aggressively in sun or light shade. Seldom at its best in small gardens for it is not by nature neat, it can be confined to island beds, pots, or trimmed as a hedge or shrub. Plumbago is a large-space ornamental that benefits from occasional heavy shearing, especially in winter when somewhat dormant. Native of South Africa, it has long been naturalized in warm dry regions. It is shown with *Bauhinia*. On page 128 it is pictured growing over a cement block wall with *Spartium junceum* (Spanish broom) and red geranium.

BEAUMONTIA GRANDIFLORA | *Apocynaceae* | 29°F.
Easter lily vine | Spring-Summer | India

Beaumontia is one of California's showiest vines. White fragrant funnelform flowers four inches across in copious clusters crown the ends of thick vining branches from mid-spring into summer. A heavy twiner with bold eight inch rich green leaves, heavily veined, this Indian liana needs heavy support, a sunny wind-sheltered exposure and some pruning after its principal flowering. It also likes deep, rich, reasonably moist, well-drained soil and lots of room to spread even when grown as a great mounded shrub with all vining ends cut off. Easter lily vine has few pests and can be grown easily from stem cuttings which bloom sooner than plants from seed.

| CLEMATIS ARMANDII | *Ranunculaceae* | 20°F. |
|---|---|---|
| Evergreen clematis | Spring | China |

Evergreen clematis is a most dramatic climber when located in moist, well-drained partially shaded spots. In early spring the dark green, prominently-veined foliage is drenched with star-like white flowers of exquisite beauty. The opposite, compound leaves are distinguished by four to eight inch leaflets. *C. armandii* twines rampantly into trees and cascades gracefully from roof or wall, and is most successful where there is at least a hint of winter. Somewhat subject to foliage die-back, it should be pruned after bloom. *C. indivisa* from New Zealand with two to three inch white flowers is a vigorous evergreen climber.

Two of the showiest deciduous clematis hybrids grown in the subtropics are *C.* X *lawsoniana* 'Henryi' (large white) and the violet *C.* X *jackmanii*. Two North American native species, *C. crispa*, with urn-shaped bluish-purple flowers, and *C. texensis*, with similar scarlet flowers, are attractive low deciduous climbers.

COMBRETUM FRUTICOSUM — *Combretaceae* — 26°F.
Summer-Fall — Tropical America

Brilliant yellow to orange flowers in groups up to four inches long by two inches wide glorify this vine in summer. The flowers somewhat resemble those of the bottle brush. This woody climber is best trained on a fence or trellis, requires little care, and does well in sunny locations. *Combretum grandiflorum* with scarlet flowers and C. *paniculatum* with very showy red flowers, both native of tropical Africa, should be tried in warmer areas.

CLYTOSTOMA CALLISTEGIOIDES
*(Bignonia violacea)*
Orchid trumpet vine

*Bignoniaceae* — 24°F.

Spring-Summer — Argentina, Brazil

Probably the most adaptable of all showy flowering climbers in southern California, the orchid trumpet vine grows easily and blooms for almost a month in sun or almost complete shade, sandy soil or clay, at the beach or far inland. It is amazingly frost-tolerant. A bit slow to start, this shiny-leaved evergreen eventually spreads 15 to 20 feet and may grow twice as high. It is rather easily controlled by copious pruning at any season. Cascading masses of three inch orchid-colored trumpet blossoms usually begin in April, climax in May and continue sporadically into autumn. It is rarely afflicted with disease or pests.

DOXANTHA UNGUIS-CATI | *Bignoniaceae* | 15°F.
Cat's claw vine | Summer | W. Indies & Tropical America

One of several yellow trumpet vines grown in the southwest, *Doxantha,* formerly known as *Bignonia tweediana,* is the hardiest of the showy self-clinging climbers. Its little claw-like appendages attach themselves to all but slickest tile to ascend at an amazing rate. Long a standby for the desert southwest, cat's claw is being used more commonly now in coastal areas where the plant is a bit slower and much easier to control. Deciduous with frost it is often nearly evergreen in mild districts. In spring its new growth is palest golden green with copper tips. Each flower is four inches across, a vibrant lemon yellow.

A one gallon-size plant installed in spring in full sun or partial shade can in six months transform an entire facade from glaring concrete to a living wall of texture and shadow pattern. This vine and lemon eucalyptus are nature's gifts to high-rise buildings and structural retainers. Once established, cat's claw is almost ineradicable and thus an efficient soil binder. Pruning may be done at any time, and it should be watered regularly.

GELSEMIUM SEMPERVIRENS | *Loganiaceae* | 15°F.
Carolina jessamine | Winter-Spring | S.E. U.S. to Central America

This is another most adaptable climber, seldom greedy and well suited to small gardens. It requires reasonably-watered locations of sun or light shade (opposite, lower left). The small funnel-form, deep yellow flowers cascade profusely from light golden-green small foliage on willowy red-brown stems almost bamboo-like in their delicacy. Established plants in warm-winter gardens may start flowering as early as Thanksgiving and continue to June with March as the high point of color. The state flower of South Carolina, *Gelsemium,* is completely hardy throughout most of southern California. Some thinning and topping after bloom are advisable. Insects and diseases are rare.

HIBBERTIA SCANDENS | *Dilleniaceae* | 28°F.
Guinea gold vine | Summer-Fall | Australia

Clear lemon-yellow single flowers, each three inches across, are displayed against glossy dark green leaves and twisting red-brown stems from late spring to mid-fall. Guinea gold (illustrated lower right), often sold as *H. volubilis,* is one of our neatest vines or ground covers. It is easily controllable, looks well the year around, and is suitable for most partially shaded moist sites. Because it is a summer bloomer one might well place hibbertia near the cool-season Carolina jessamine. Avoid locations with reflected heat or drought else thrips can be a real problem; hose off leaves often in warm dry weather. Allow 15 feet minimum spread and prune top hard after flowering.

DISTICTIS X RIVERSII | *Bignoniaceae* | 28°F.

Royal trumpet vine | Summer-Fall

Four-inch mauve to royal purple trumpets, with yellow to orange throats, abundantly crown the branch ends of *Distictis* X *riversii,* one of the subtropic's showiest and most vigorous warm-weather bloomers. This hybrid between *Distictis laxiflora* and *D. buccinatoria* (red trumpet vine) bears abundant shining dark leaves almost identical to those of the latter species. Sun-loving, intolerant of much frost, resistant to pests and disease, this vine grows easily and well in most fast-draining soils with average moisture.

*Distictis laxiflora,* the vanilla-scented trumpet vine from Mexico, is also a popular summer-blooming species in southern California. Its three and one-half inch flowers are purple, turning orchid to white, the foliage lighter green and less lustrous than that of *D.* X *riversii.* Also the vine is less vigorous but is choice for sunny, windless sites. Prune both species as flowers wane.

MANDEVILLA 'ALICE DU PONT' *Apocynaceae* 33°F.
Summer

This aristocratic summer-blooming tropical climber of border-line hardiness in California has loose racemes of clearest pink funnel-form flowers with vivid crimson throats framed by deeply veined leathery dark green leaves. The first plant of this hybrid grown out of doors in California has thrived for several years on a partially sunny fence with average care and watering at the UCLA Botanical Garden. Some of its leaves fall during winter but it is essentially evergreen. It should be limited to the very mildest sites having considerable accumulated warmth. Any pruning must be done in warm weather. It must be set fairly high in fast-draining soil as a cold wet root-run is lethal.

*Mandevilla suaveolens,* Chilean jasmine, is a 20 foot white-flowered vine. *M. splendens* 'Profusa,' formerly listed as *Dipladenia,* is a smaller six foot vine with rose-pink flowers. Both bloom in summer.

GLORIOSA ROTHSCHILDIANA | *Liliaceae* | 25°F.
GLORIOSA SUPERBA

Gloriosa lily | Summer-Fall | Tropical Africa

These tuberous-rooted climbing lilies are uncommon in California but they are occasionally grown outside and are hardier than usually considered. They die back after flowering in summer and early fall and remain dormant all winter. They thrive only in warm-summer gardens, in full sun or partial shade, in soil that drains fast and dries out during dormancy. In very wet winters covering may be necessary. The leaves are prolonged into tendrils, the three inch lily flowers solitary in the leaf axils. Many blossoms may be produced by each adult tuber, and new tubers should grow from existing ones each season.

*G. rothschildiana* has crimson to scarlet flowers, yellow and whitish at base, the segments wavy-margined and reflexed. The flowers of *G. superba* are yellow changing to red, the segments narrow and crisp.

OXERA PULCHELLA | *Verbenaceae* | 30°F.
Oxera | Variable | New Caledonia

Another distinguished tropical for gardens of the adventuresome is oxera, an evergreen climber from New Caledonia with conspicuous white two inch lightly-scented flowers further characterized by long spider-like stamens, and oppositely assembled evergreen leaves. The blossoming time is extremely variable, February, August or October, and some years not at all. Less sensitive to cold than *Petrea* or *Mandevilla* 'Alice du Pont' this vining shrub is still touchy to frost so it should be placed on warmest walls away from prevailing wind, in fast-draining soil with ample humus. Only occasionally is oxera in the trade but it is well worth hunting and trying to bloom. Any pruning must be accomplished in warm weather. The red blossom shown with oxera is *Euphorbia fulgens*, a species rarely grown in California.

| HARDENBERGIA COMPTONIANA | *Leguminosae* | 24°F. |
|---|---|---|
| Lilac vine | Winter-Spring | Australia |

This is one of the numerous Australian pea vines, a hardy evergreen open subject for pattern work on lightly-shaded fences or spilling over retaining walls. Its small violet to lilac or even pink or white flowers cascade profusely in late winter and spring. This pea vine rarely grows as rampantly as *H. violacea*, a coarser inferior subject often sold as *H. comptoniana*. However it is not foolproof for it often tangles, and it requires regular pruning of ungainly side branches especially after blooming. Frequent hosing off will lessen the occurrence of thrips which may disfigure foliage in rainless months.

| LONICERA HILDEBRANDIANA | *Caprifoliaceae* | 30°F. |
|---|---|---|
| Burmese honeysuckle | Summer-Fall | Burma |

Cream-white blossoms, up to seven inches long, that age yellow to gold distinguish this giant Burmese, the largest of our many honeysuckles. The flowers occur abundantly in clusters and emit their familiar fragrance. Leaves are roundish to oval, shiningly evergreen, tender to frost. The plant grows rapidly and strong (to 30 feet) in sun or light shade. Its limitations in addition to size are littering leaves that often yellow before falling, heavy twining stems often bare at the base and a fairly invasive root system. Strong support is necessary. It is perhaps best trained horizontally on heavy wires and replaced when it becomes too bare and woody. Prune almost continually in warm weather, never in cold.

*Lonicera sempervirens* 'Superba,' trumpet honeysuckle, native of the eastern U.S. is grown for its scarlet and yellow flowers. The hybrid with *L. americana, L.* X *heckrottii,* with purple and yellow fragrant flowers, is a fine garden form.

PASSIFLORA | *Passifloraceae* | 25°F.
Passion vine | Summer | South America

At least seven passion vines are in cultivation in California, all relatively easy to grow and reasonably hardy. *Passiflora* X *alato-caerulea (P. pfordtii),* shown on page 95, is the most frequently seen. Its foliage is fairly free of predators except the caterpillar. Flowers are white-with-orchid and a crown of deep blue, purple and white. The blossoms of *P. caerulea* (illustrated opposite) are similar but smaller but the plant is more invasive and prone to caterpillars. *P. edulis* is more or less deciduous, tender and often homely, grown exclusively for its fruits. *P. jamesonii,* a most beautiful salmon to coral, is sensational in Carmel but rarely thrives south of Santa Barbara. All passion vines need pruning after flowering and occasional spraying for caterpillars. Also tender are *P. coccinea* and *P. manicata* (lower left) with scarlet flowers with royal blue crowns. The long-tubed clear light pink blossoms of *P. mollissima* are profuse. Its invasiveness makes it desirable for cliffs and screening waste places. *P. racemosa (P. princeps)* (lower right) is perhaps the aristocrat with pendent trusses of soft rose to coral, long-tubed blossoms. It is best where humidity is fairly high.

SOLANDRA MAXIMA | *Solanaceae* | 30°F.
Cup of gold (copa de oro) | Fall-Winter | Mexico

This luxuriant climber has large yellow coconut-scented flowers and smooth green leaves. It was long grown as *Solandra guttata, S. nitida* or *S. hartwegii.* The flowers open light yellow and turn to gold (illustrated on page 95 with passion vine, nasturtium and geranium). *S. longiflora,* from the West Indies, is easily distinguished by its long-tubed cream-white flowers that turn pale yellow. Both have deep brown-purple markings. True *S. guttata* has conspicuously woolly leaves.

All solandras are tender lianas, burly-stemmed, rampant, for large gardens and sturdy arbors. The blossoms are magnificent and may occur at any season, especially in winter. *S. longiflora* is usually showiest in November. All need considerable moisture, part to full sun, lots of room and a near frostless site not far from the ocean. All may be pruned hard in warm weather.

| DISTICTIS BUCCINATORIA | *Bignoniaceae* | 27°F. |
|---|---|---|
| Red trumpet vine | Spring-Summer | Mexico |

Long familiar in California gardens as *Bignonia cherere* and *Phaedranthus buccinatorius* the red trumpet vine is known for its copious clusters of large funnelform blossoms that open orange-red with yellow throats and age to rose-red before dropping. Bloom normally occurs from April through summer, usually most generously in locations not far from the sea. The foliage is dark green, shining and fairly pest free. The plant is extremely robust, the top growth heavy, so it needs strong support and hard pruning after flowering. Largest flowers in greatest numbers nearly always occur on the largest leaved plants, so propagation from cuttings is desirable. A very large and handsome specimen may be seen at Huntington Gardens.

| PODRANEA RICASOLIANA | *Bignoniaceae* | 32°F. |
|---|---|---|
| | Summer | South Africa |

Another trumpet vine, this one pink-striped crimson—uncommon but occasionally sold as *Bignonia mackenii*—is most frequent in the southwest corner of the state, especially La Jolla. Lacy foliage of considerable refinement drops with a hint of frost. Carefully pruned *P. ricasoliana* can be stunning in summer spilling from an arbor or off hot rocks.

Even rarer is a winter-blooming cousin, *P. brycei*, with large clusters of pale pink fragrant flowers marbled red with yellow throats. Leaves are deciduous and the plant tender.

PYROSTEGIA VENUSTA | *Bignoniaceae* | 28°F.
Flame vine | Fall-Winter | Brazil-Paraguay

Strictly for hottest gardens with reflected heat, this climber, also sold as *P. ignea* and *Bignonia venusta*, reaches its climax in Palm Springs and the south about Christmas time. Especially happy on tile roofs whose color is convivial with the sheets of flame-orange narrow-tubed flowers that obliterate the usually sparse foliage, flame vine drips brilliantly from eaves and can curtain concrete walls that face the sun. Hopeless in shade and dubious in most of the fog belt *Pyrostegia* is sensational when happily sited. Any pruning is best accomplished in warmest weather.

SENECIO ANGULATUS | *Compositae* | 25°F.
Fall, Winter | South Africa

SENECIO CONFUSUS | 32°F.
Spring to Fall | Mexico

Two of the numerous climbing senecios are *S. angulatus* and *S. confusus* (opposite, lower left). *S. confusus* blooms red-orange from May into October with thickish bright green leaves. Best in coastal gardens with fairly moist air and no frost, it also appreciates its roots in some shade, its top in half a day's sun. Keeping old flower heads cut is a chore but worth the effort. Cut the whole vine back hard when through blooming; it is slightly dormant in winter.

The somewhat succulent *S. angulatus* (lower right) is yellow, with shining evergreen leaves. It is shown with *Solanum dulcamaroides*, violet with yellow centers, and red cotoneaster berries.

STEPHANOTIS FLORIBUNDA | *Asclepiadaceae* | 32°F.
Madagascar jasmine | Late Summer | Madagascar

The enduring elegance of form, texture and fragrance in *Stephanotis* is rivaled in few ornamentals. Each two inch blossom is composed of five waxen petals that flare from an ivory tube. The flowers cluster loosely in groups of five to nine, startling white against shining dark green leaves (see upper left), in late summer.

Successful placement means shaded roots, head in at least half sun, moist rich soil that drains fast. Sandy loam with redwood shavings and leafmold provides an ideal growing medium. On a wind-sheltered wall this plant's well-groomed appearance is a delight at all seasons. But it can be damaged by frost, and water-logged ground will shorten its naturally long life. Light feeding and any pruning should be done in warm weather.

STIGMAPHYLLON LITTORALE | *Malpighiaceae* | 26°F.
Orchid vine | Spring-Fall | Brazil

The orchid vine, *Stigmaphyllon littorale*, shown upper right, is more rugged than its slender twining relative from the West Indies, *S. ciliatum*. Its larger, darker green leaves are somewhat hairy and coarse. The lemon-yellow, green-tinged, conspicuously clustered flowers are produced recurrently over many months. Excellent on hot banks where the robust tuberous roots can check erosion, this species will cover chain link fences. *S. ciliatum* is a lighter-weight vine blooming profusely and intermittently from spring to fall, with exquisite small clear yellow flowers suggesting little orchids in form. It should be planted in well-aerated soil with ample humus. Prune in warm season.

TRACHELOSPERMUM JASMINOIDES | *Apocynaceae* | 15°F.
Star jasmine | Spring-Summer | China

Star jasmine (shown in the lower picture opposite) is one of the commonest and most versatile among evergreen twiners. It serves either as a vine, a low shrub or a ground cover, and is hardy. Its white lacy star-like flowers, enchantingly fragrant, are profuse in spring and summer, and contrast handsomely with dark green polished two inch leaves. By nature a rambler, the plant may be trained to curtain walls, spill from plant boxes, climb posts and cover fences and eaves. A bit slow to start, its life span is long. Shear unwanted tendrils at any season.

*Trachelospermum asiaticum*, the yellow star jasmine from Japan and Korea, is a rarer species with slightly broader leaves. It is less vigorous and grows more slowly.

The genus *Jasminum*, in the olive family, contains a number of the true jasmines. *J. angulare* from South Africa (erroneously known in California as *J. azoricum*) has white flowers from summer to winter, likes a sunny location and is frost tender at 30°F. *J. humile* 'Revolutum,' the yellow bush jasmine from tropical Asia, will withstand cold to 10°F., blooms in summer, likes a sunny location and achieves a height of 10 feet when used as a shrub. The primrose jasmine from China, *J. mesnyi (J. primulinum)*, is also hardy, has yellow flowers from November to April, likes a partially shaded location and will extend to 15 feet. The Spanish jasmine (actually from Iran), *J. grandiflorum*, grows to 15 feet, has white flowers in the summer, is hardy to 28°F. and also likes partial shade. The Chinese jasmine, *J. polyanthum*, grows to 20 feet, has fragrant white blossoms, rose-colored outside, blooms from February through July, likes a partially shaded, moist location and is somewhat more tender.

| SOLANUM WENDLANDII | *Solanaceae* | 25°F. |
|---|---|---|
| Costa Rican nightshade | Summer | Costa Rica |

In hot protected sites *Solanum wendlandii* produces a summer spectacle of lavender-blue two and one-half inch blossoms in large branched clusters, yellow-eyed and conspicuously handsome. Though best in full sun in protected coastal areas, it may flower inland when grown in part shade. It should be pruned immediately after flowering. Deciduous during cold weather.

*Solanum jasminoides*, the white sweet-potato vine, is hardy to 20°, has bluish-white, small, star-shaped, yellow-centered flowers which occur intermittently all year, sometimes sparingly, sometimes in cascades. It is best in slight shade with moisture and occasional heavy pruning at any season.

*Solanum dulcamaroides (S. macrantherum)* is shown on page 121 growing with yellow *Senecio angulatus* and red cotoneaster berries. It is an exquisite climber with long-stemmed emerald to light green foliage, graceful twining branches and yellow-centered, vividly violet flowers, conspicuously clustered. Little red berry-like fruits follow the bloom which may occur at any season. A wind-sheltered sunny location is best.

| WISTERIA SINENSIS | *Leguminosae* | 10°F. |
|---|---|---|
| Chinese wisteria | Spring | China |

The wisterias, appreciated for their striking pendulous clusters of pea-like blossoms in spring, are large, deciduous vines for sun or partial shade. Flower buds are encouraged with periodic pruning after flowering which will also restrain these vigorous vines to moderate size. They may even be trained as shrubs or small trees. Root pruning may be necessary to shock plants into setting flower buds.

The Chinese wisteria, illustrated opposite, has fat clusters of lilac or white blossoms. The Japanese wisteria, *W. floribunda*, produces hanging flower clusters one and a half feet long, its cultivar 'Longissima' skeins to four feet. The silky wisteria, *W. venusta*, has white flowers, and its cultivar 'Violacea' fragrant purple-blue flowers in short heavy clusters.

THUNBERGIA GREGORII | *Acanthaceae* | 30°F.
| All Year | Africa

*Thunbergia gregorii*, upper picture, and *T. gibsonii* are light-weight climbers or crawlers grown for their curtains of brilliant orange blooms in full sun, mostly in summer and fall. *T. gregorii* with richer evergreen, somewhat hairy foliage blooms heavily in hot weather and often throughout the year. Other somewhat similar thunbergias are *T. mysorensis* from India which produces yellow and reddish flowers opening in succession along the pendent thread-like flower stems. The black-eyed clockvine, *T. alata*, is known for its variable flower colors, white to orange or even maroon with shiny black centers.

*Thunbergia grandiflora*, the blue sky vine from India (lower right), has ropes and skeins of light blue, two-lipped funnels dangling from pale green leaf masses in autumn. This plant should be pruned back hard after blooming. Any frost will blacken the six inch leaves but recovery is rapid in the spring. Creditable flowering requires months of accumulated heat. The leaves are subject to yellowing. This is no plant for limited spaces but grown on a large and sturdy arbor it can be dramatic. A white-flowered variety is also available. All thunbergias should be placed in sunny locations in deep porous soil away from wind, and pruned only in warm weather.

TECOMARIA CAPENSIS | *Bignoniaceae* | 25°F.
Cape honeysuckle | Summer-Fall | South Africa

This is a rapid-growing evergreen vining shrub (see lower left) with lustrous dark green leaves handsome at all seasons. It flowers brilliantly in sun through summer and fall with upright clusters of red-orange tubular funnels. *Tecomaria* grows well in dry or wet soils of sand or heaviest clay and functions in the garden as a bush, vine or ground cover. Heavy pruning in early winter after most of bloom is past should keep it from being invasive, but it can be cut again at any time. From seashore to desert it is completely successful and usually free from pests and disease. It will even thrive in shade though it seldom blooms there. There is also a yellow-flowered form, less vigorous with fewer smaller blossoms.

*Plumbago auriculata*

See page 1

## ADDITIONAL VINING PLANTS OF MERIT

Including spillers and sprawlers for low walls, and wall shrubs which can be used as vines if supported.
Where temperature is not given the plants are usually grown as annuals.

| Species | Family | Common Name | Origin | Height to | Color | Season of Color | Hardy to | Placement |
|---|---|---|---|---|---|---|---|---|
| Abutilon megapotamicum | Malvaceae | flowering maple | Brazil | 10′ | yellow & red | April-September | 25° | shade |
| Araujia sericofera | Asclepiadaceae | white bladder flower | So. America | 40′ | white | May-November | 27° | sun |
| Begonia scandens | Begoniaceae | climbing begonia | Trop. America | 6′ | white | winter, spring | 35° | shade |
| B. coccinea, B. corallina | | | Trop. America | 10′ | pink, red | almost all year | | shade |
| Bignonia capreolata | Bignoniaceae | trumpet flower | So. U.S. | 50′ | orange-red | spring, summer | 10° | partial shade |
| Bomarea caldasiana | Amaryllidaceae | | Trop. America | 15′ | red & yellow | spring-fall | 27° | shade |
| Campsis grandiflora | Bignoniaceae | Chinese trumpet creeper | China | 30′ | scarlet | July-September | –30° | sun |
| C. radicans | | trumpet creeper | Eastern U.S. | 50′ | orange, scarlet | summer | –30° | sun |
| C. X tagliabuana 'Mme. Galen' | | | garden hybrid | 30′ | salmon red | summer | –30° | sun |
| Camptosema rubicundum *(Dioclea glycinoides)* | Leguminosae | | Argentina | | red | summer | 25° | sun |
| Chonemorpha fragrans *(C. macrophylla)* | Apocynaceae | | S.E. Asia | 30′ | white | summer | 27° | sun |
| Clerodendrum thomsoniae | Verbenaceae | glory bower | W. Africa | 15′ | white & red | May-September | 35° | partial shade |
| Clianthus puniceus | Leguminosae | parrot's beak | New Zealand | 8′ | crimson | June, July | | sun or partial shade |
| Cobaea scandens | Polemoniaceae | cup & saucer vine | Mexico | 20′ | violet | July-October | 24° | sun |
| Cymbalaria muralis | Scrophulariaceae | Kenilworth ivy | Europe | 3′ | lilac-blue | spring-fall | | shade |
| Dolichos lignosus | Leguminosae | Australian pea vine | Australia | | white or violet | summer | 24° | sun |
| Eccremocarpus scaber | Bignoniaceae | Chilean glory flower | Chile | 12′ | orange-red | summer | | sun or partial shade |
| Heterocentron elegans *(Schizocentron)* | Melasto-mataceae | Spanish shawl | Mexico, Guatemala | prostrate | purple or violet | summer | 27° | partial shade |
| Holmskioldia sanguinea | Verbenaceae | Chinese hat plant | Himalayas | 20′ | terra cotta | almost all year | 30° | sun or partial shade |
| Hoya carnosa | Asclepiadaceae | wax vine | Australia | 15′ | dusty pink | spring, summer | 28° | partial shade |
| Hylocereus undatus | Cactaceae | night-blooming cereus | Trop. America | 40′ | white | July-October at **two week intervals** | 28° | sun or partial shade |

| | | | | | | | | |
|---|---|---|---|---|---|---|---|---|
| Ipomoea acuminata leari | Convolvulaceae | blue dawn flower | Trop. America | 30′ | bright blue | spring-fall | | sun |
| I. alba *(Calonyction)* | | moon flower | Tropics | 40′ | white | summer-fall | | sun |
| I. coccinea *(Quamoclit)* | | scarlet star | Arizona & New Mexico | 10′ | scarlet | July-October | | sun or partial shade |
| Jacquemontia pentantha | Convolvulaceae | | Florida-So. America | 10′ | bright blue | spring | 30° | sun or partial shade |
| Kennedia prostrata | Leguminosae | coral pea | Australia | prostrate | scarlet | early summer | | sun |
| Lablab purpureus *(Dolichos lablab)* | Leguminosae | hyacinth bean | Tropics | 25′ | purple or white | summer | 30° | sun |
| Lapageria rosea | Liliaceae | Chilean bellflower | Chile | 12′ | rose-red | summer, fall | 15° | shade |
| Lathyrus odoratus | Leguminosae | sweet pea | Italy | 8′ | all but blue | spring, summer | | sun |
| Lopezia hirsuta *(L. albiflora)* | Onagraceae | mosquito plant | Mexico | prostrate | white, pink | spring-fall | 30° | partial shade |
| Macfadyena dentata *(Anemopaegma chamberlaynii* of trade) | Bignoniaceae | yellow trumpet vine | Brazil | 30′ | yellow | summer | 30° | sun |
| Manettia bicolor | Rubiaceae | manettia | Brazil | 6′ | scarlet, yellow tip | summer | 32° | partial shade |
| Maurandya barclaiana | Scrophulariaceae | maurandia | Mexico | 10′ | purple, violet | spring-fall | 32° | sun |
| M. erubescens | | | Mexico | 10′ | rose red | spring-fall | 32° | sun |
| Mina lobata *(Quamoclit)* | Convolvulaceae | Spanish flag | Mexico | 20′ | red turning yellow & white | summer | 25° | sun |
| Pandorea jasminoides | Bignoniaceae | bower vine | Australia | 30′ | white, pink | June-October | 30° | sun |
| Pereskia aculeata | Cactaceae | lemon vine | Trop. America | 30′ | white, pink, yellow | summer & intermittent | 32° | sun |
| Petrea volubilis | Verbenaceae | queen's wreath | Trop. America | 25′ | lavender-dark blue | spring, summer | 32° | sun |
| Phaseolus coccineus | Leguminosae | scarlet runner bean | Mexico, So. America | 20′ | scarlet | summer | 32° | sun |
| Philadelphus mexicanus | Saxifragaceae | mock-orange | Mexico | 15′ | white | summer | 22° | sun |
| Pithecoctenium echinatum | Bignoniaceae | monkey comb | Trop. America | | white | summer | 30° | sun |
| Polygonum aubertii | Polygonaceae | silver-lace vine | China | 30′ | greenish white | June-September | 20° | sun |
| Selenicereus grandiflorus | Cactaceae | queen of the night | Jamaica, Cuba | | white, salmon outside | | 30° | sun |
| Sollya fusiformis | Pittosporaceae | blue bell creeper | Australia | 6′ | blue | spring-fall | 25° | sun |
| Tropaeolum majus | Tropaeolaceae | nasturtium | Mexico, So. America | 15′ | all but blue | summer, fall | 32° | sun or partial shade |
| T. speciosum | | | Chile | | vermilion, yellow | summer, fall | 32° | sun or partial shade |

# FLOWERING PLANTS FOR COLOR ON THE GROUND

See page 154 *Drosanthemum* spp.

# *Chapter IV*

# FLOWERING PLANTS FOR COLOR ON THE GROUND

The plants in this chapter are those which can be used as ground covers, defined here as plants which can add color to the landscape near ground level, especially when planted in mass. Effective use of color can be achieved with annuals, biennials, perennials, many types of succulents, vines, and low shrubs. Many different types of plants can be massed to make excellent ground covers.

Ground covers have several functional values in addition to the color emphasized here. They serve as a method for weed control; add texture in the composition of landscape design; soften the effect of cliffs or other rugged abutments; control erosion, particularly on slopes; can provide a fire-retardant border; and serve as substitutes for lawns. When low maintenance is a consideration, low, spreading ground covers are the answer. It should be emphasized that additional ground covers are to be found in the chapters on shrubs, vines and California native plants.

CATHARANTHUS ROSEUS *Apocynaceae* 27°F.
*(Vinca rosea)*
Madagascar periwinkle Spring-Fall Tropics

This perennial shown opposite is treated as a low bushy annual bedding plant in colder areas. In milder zones where it is handled as a perennial it may not be attractive in the winter but will be a mass of bloom, like the illustration, through the spring, summer and fall. Ordinarily, the foliage is a handsome glossy green and the flowers are available in a variety of color patterns of white and rose. This plant loves heat and is best in sun or light shade. It is often used as a bedding plant in parks.

*Catharanthus roseus*

DIMORPHOTHECA and OSTEOSPERMUM *Compositae* 20°F.
African daisies Spring-Summer South Africa

The closely related dimorphothecas and osteospermums are popular garden plants and many of their cultivars can be used effectively as ground covers. The cultivar illustrated and known as *D.* 'Buttersweet' may be a hybrid between *Dimorphotheca* and *Osteospermum*. It has shrubby growth to two and a half feet and benefits from occasional hard pruning.

*Osteospermum fruticosum,* the trailing African daisy, shown upper right, is characterized by quick trailing growth and purplish flowers which appear in winter and spring. The typical wild form is said to have white flowers. The rather fleshy leaves are light green and plants reach one and a half feet in height. 'Snow White' is a selection with more upright growth and nearly white flowers.

In 1967 the Los Angeles Arboretum made another selection called *Osteospermum* 'Burgundy Mound,' shown upper left. This forms cushion-shaped plants with wine-colored ray flowers. All of these forms require full sun and will tolerate only light traffic. (The bronze-leafed plant in the center of the upper right picture is New Zealand Flax, *Phormium tenax*).

*Dimorphotheca annua,* Cape marigold from South Africa, is a 16 inch annual plant with white and violet flowers during the winter. *D. sinuata,* another South African annual daisy, grows to only 12 inches and produces orange-yellow flowers in winter and spring.

## POTENTILLA CRANTZII *(P. verna)*

Spring cinquefoil

| | |
|---|---|
| *Rosaceae* | 0°F. |
| Spring-Summer | Europe |

The spring cinquefoil is valuable for its adaptability to many climates. It is a low creeper with clusters of bright yellow flowers in spring and summer, making a dense ground cover which spreads rapidly by runners in sunny locations having well-drained soil. It is an excellent cover for dry slopes. *Potentilla cinerea,* alpine cinquefoil, with pale yellow flowers and *P. tridentata,* the wineleaf cinquefoil, with white flowers are also hardy.

AJUGA REPTANS | *Labiatae* | 15°F.
Bugle weed | Spring-Summer | Europe

Ajuga is one of the most satisfactory ground covers for shade, but will endure some sun in coastal areas if moisture is adequate. It will withstand occasional light foot traffic and will spread and cover well from a thin planting. A number of interesting cultivars are available. 'Purpurea' has bronzy purple leaves which provide a strong note of color for the landscape designer. 'Variegata' has white-edged leaves. A giant-leaved form, *A. reptans* 'Crispa,' is also available. This plant is not sensitive to frost. Attractive blue flowers appear on the spikes in spring and early summer.

CONVOLVULUS SABATIUS MAURITANICUS | *Convolvulaceae* | 15°F.
Ground morning glory | Spring-Summer | North Africa

Blooming for a long period during the spring and extending into the warmer months of the year, this attractive low-growing perennial plant has hairy gray-green leaves and bluish-lavender flowers. It requires a well-drained soil and the plants should be thinned out occasionally to encourage new growth. It is useful in both solid masses and mixed plantings and is particularly good for hot, dry situations. This convolvulus is grown in many areas of California and is also usable as a hanging basket plant.

In this photograph taken at Corona del Mar the low marigolds provide a color contrast to the blue of *Convolvulus.*

*Convolvulus cneorum,* a four foot shrub with white flowers, blooms from May to September in full sun with fast drainage.

POLYGONUM CAPITATUM | *Polygonaceae* | 28°F.
All Year | Japan

Characterized by abundant small pink flower heads and a bronzy foliage, this attractive knotweed (in foreground above), has been popular in the mild climate areas because it requires little attention and is colorful throughout the year. Somewhat weedy, it is best in isolated areas where it can be confined and where there will be no foot traffic. Often it will reseed itself naturally after a freeze. It is an attractive plant when draped over a wall.

AGAPANTHUS AFRICANUS | *Liliaceae* | 23°F.
Lily-of-the-Nile | Summer | South Africa

The common name of this blue-flowering plant, shown in the left of the above photo, is misleading since it does not come from the northern part of Africa. It does, however, prefer abundant watering when in flower, as the name might suggest. A wide selection of agapanthus species and cultivars is available, varying in size, habit, and color of flower. There are both deciduous and evergreen, and dwarf and tall types, and colors range from white to blue and purple. These plants produce cut flowers for spectacular flower arrangements. They are adaptable to many locations and particularly effective as container plants in the patio.

The large plant on the right is *Doryanthes palmeri*, a native of Australia, which puts forth a tall spike of red flowers resembling the torch ginger.

## ARCTOTHECA CALENDULA

Cape gold

| *Compositae* | 28°F. |
| --- | --- |
| Spring-Winter | South Africa |

Extremely vigorous, *Arctotheca* quickly spreads by rooting stolons. With water and if unchecked a small plant can cover as much as 200 square feet in a year or two. It should be introduced with caution to areas having frost-free winters and rainy summers. Fortunately only a single self-sterile clone has been introduced to southern California and it therefore cannot spread by seeds.

The mat of silvery green leaves varies in thickness according to availability of water. In sunny places large bright yellow flowers are produced profusely most of the year. Coarse and not as refined as many ground covers, Cape gold is best used to cover large slopes where less robust plants need not compete with it.

## PRIMULA X POLYANTHA

English primrose

| *Primulaceae* | 20°F. |
| --- | --- |
| Winter-Spring | Europe |

The English primroses are notable examples of the progress made by plant breeders. Many unusual types with a wide variety of flower colors, ranging through the spectrum, are available in the seed trade. They are one of the best bedding plants for a mass display of color in shaded areas. *Primula* plants may remain in the ground several years before it is necessary to divide the clumps and start them over. They make excellent cut flowers or potted plants and are a favorite the world over in window boxes. Moist well-mulched slightly acid soil is required, and plants must be protected against slugs and snails.

FRAGARIA CHILOENSIS | *Rosaceae* | 10°F.
Wild strawberry, sand strawberry | Spring-Summer | Pacific Coast, North and South America

This wild strawberry of new world origin has leaves of a deep shiny green. It has been widely used as a lawn substitute where only light foot traffic may be expected. In the fall, the leaves take on attractive reddish tones (upper left).

Occasional mowing, especially early in the season, will improve the quality of the cover. Although this strawberry is somewhat drought-resistant, it is best with watering and fertilizing. However, overwatering may cause attacks of disease and good drainage is important. Iron sulfate is used to control chlorosis (yellowing of the foliage). Occasional replanting is desirable as the plants get older.

Fruiting is ordinarily sparse but the introduction from Rancho Santa Ana Botanic Garden, 'Hybrid No. 25,' is similar to the species and produces some usable strawberries. This cultivar should be kept thinned to favor production of fruit.

CERASTIUM TOMENTOSUM | *Caryophyllaceae* | 0°F.
Snow-in-summer | Spring-Summer | Europe

This low creeping hardy perennial is frequently used in rock gardens and borders in the colder parts of the country. Abundant white flowers appear in spring and summer, their color enhanced by grayish, hairy foliage. The plant prefers sun, spreads rapidly in favorable situations, and some trimming is needed when it is grown for several years. It is valuable for cold mountain areas. (Shown upper right).

The effectiveness of *Cerastium* may be enhanced by contrasting materials such as a clumping grass, the blue fescue, *Festuca glauca,* shown with it. This hardy plant requires well-drained soil and some sun for best results.

CENTRANTHUS RUBER | *Valerianaceae* | 15°F.
Jupiter's beard, valerian | Spring-Fall | Mediterranean area

Here is a horticultural Cinderella which can become a glamorous fairy princess when used in the right setting! It is slightly weedy but not objectionably invasive and it will give a lavish display of color over long periods with very little water and care. It can be used boldly in large masses, for this is an ideal low-maintenance plant. It is benefited by occasional thinning but will persist year after year in the same location. This is a good plant for steep, dry slopes and unfavorable soils. The flowers range from various reds and pinks to a pure white and are produced in profusion over a long period of time.

The effective but informal use of this plant in front of a 100 year old building in Cambria is illustrated in the lower photograph on the opposite page.

| ECHIUM FASTUOSUM | *Boraginaceae* | 22°F. |
|---|---|---|
| Pride of Madeira | Spring | Canary Islands |

Bold plants which produce spectacular foliage or flower effects can be used as ground covers, especially on slopes, as the photo demonstrates. This unusual plant has irregular spreading stems and large spikes to six feet of purple or dark blue flowers which are produced in late spring above the foliage. The plant requires little care or watering and is especially good near the seacoast, but it thrives well in the Pasadena area. Structural forms can be developed by pruning. It can be used effectively against a hedge or wall. Some closely related species with different flower colors are available. Individual plants may not be long-lived, but they reproduce readily from self-sown seedlings.

FELICIA AMELLOIDES 'SANTA ANITA' | *Compositae* | 20°F.
Blue daisy, agathea | Spring-Fall | Africa

This new cultivar of the old garden favorite, the blue African daisy, was developed at the Los Angeles Arboretum by increasing the chromosomes of the plant through treatment with colchicine. This increased the flower size and substance considerably. It is worthy both as a ground cover in the garden and as a cut flower. (Lower left). 'San Gabriel" is more shrubby. New cultivars include 'Jolly,' 'Dwarf,' and 'Elisabeth Marshall.'

FELICIA FRUTICOSA | *Compositae* | 26°F.
Aster bush | Spring | South Africa

The bush aster (earlier placed in *Aster* or *Diplopappus*) is a somewhat woody plant with a height and spread of several feet and rather fine but dense foliage. In the spring it is spectacular with the entire shrub covered with purplish-blue flowers. Some thinning out of the old growth is advisable to keep the plant attractive throughout the year. The plant likes sun and requires little water. (Shown lower right).

## EUPHORBIA RIGIDA *(E. biglandulosa)*

*Euphorbiaceae* 20°F.
Winter-Spring Mediterranean area

This low growing herbaceous perennial produces attractive chartreuse-colored flower clusters at the top of stems with gray-green leaves in late winter. It is a good plant for those who prize unusual effects or who want a variety of materials for floral arrangements. After flowering, new stems appear and the old stems should be removed to maintain the best appearance at all times of the year.

## HEUCHERA

Alum root, coral bells

*Saxifragaceae* 10°F.
Summer North America

*Heuchera sanguinea* and its cultivars are well known garden favorites in a genus that includes species from various parts of North America. A few of these species are California natives, and some hybrid forms of these produced in recent years at Rancho Santa Ana Botanic Garden are particularly showy.

These plants are good in shade and prefer moist soils. They form low mounds of attractive leaves and bear beautiful panicles of red, pink, or white flowers in the summer. They are unusually graceful plants in the garden and also provide colorful cut flowers. Heucheras are easily propagated by division.

Heucheras are shown here with *Artemisia pycnocephala* and *Nemophila maculata.*

GAZANIA 'COPPER KING' *Compositae* 27°F.
Spring-Fall South Africa

Gazanias provide a colorful ground cover for areas free of foot traffic. They are best suited to warm sunny situations and do not endure prolonged freezing. Hybridizers have greatly extended the color range available to include from white and yellow to pink, orange and brownish-red, of which the popular variety 'Copper King' is an example.

Most of the older cultivars were derived from species which have a clumping habit. These spread slowly and need to be planted about a foot apart to make a solid effect. In recent years trailing types from *Gazania uniflora* have been introduced. These grow rapidly and produce long stolons which permit a few plants to spread quickly over large areas. This species has somewhat woolly foliage.

| KNIPHOFIA UVARIA | *Liliaceae* | 20°F. |
|---|---|---|
| Torch lily, redhot poker | Spring-Summer | South Africa |

*Kniphofia*, formerly called *Tritoma*, somewhat resemble the aloes in flower form. There are about 70 species of these herbaceous perennial plants, native to eastern and South Africa. Hybridization has produced a striking array of colors including white, chartreuse, yellow, gold, bright orange and flaming red. They are superb as cut flowers for their long-lasting quality, also frequent cutting stimulates flower production. The foliage is an attractive clump of long arching lily-like leaves varying in size.

Small plants with dainty spikes one foot high make excellent borders. Others produce spikes as high as six feet. Modern hybrids are robust and do not require staking. By planting a variety of cultivars, the flowering season may be extended from early spring through summer with individual plants having as many as 10 to 15 flower spikes.

Full sun and rich well-drained soil with moderate watering is all that is required. They respond well to standard commercial fertilizers and are remarkably free of pests. They can be subdivided annually in late fall or early spring. Seeds are easily germinated and the young plants will bloom the following year. For the amateur hybridizer, *Kniphofia* offers an exciting challenge as the various species cross readily and plants grown from the seed thus produced vary widely. Dr. Victor Newcomer developed a large collection of new introductions and hybrids which may be seen at the Los Angeles Arboretum.

| STRELITZIA REGINAE | *Musaceae* | 24°F. |
| --- | --- | --- |
| Bird-of-paradise | Fall-Spring | South Africa |

Unique in color and structure, this striking flower is the official city flower of Los Angeles. It is highly recommended for areas without frost. The plants vary considerably from seed and are best purchased when in bloom for color selection. They propagate readily by division and are easy to grow, preferably in full sun with a high level of fertilization, and can be adapted to container growing. The flowers are long-lasting when cut. Plants bloom about six months starting in mid-fall.

A tree-like species is *Strelitzia nicolai* with bluish and white flower petals.

LANTANA MONTEVIDENSIS — *Verbenaceae* — 26°F.

Trailing lantana — All Year — South America

This species of lantana has long trailing stems with small leaves and bears clusters of lavender-purple flowers in profusion throughout the entire year. It is considered tender but is sometimes seen in interior valleys in sheltered locations. It stands much drought and neglect and is one of the most satisfactory and ornamental plants for slopes in areas with a favorable climate. It is best in full sun and is attractive when draped over a wall. An undesirable wild seedling form should be avoided as it is an invasive weed. For a spectacular bloom over a whole year it is difficult to surpass the bush or trailing lantanas.

Flowering aloes and yellow *Cassia artemisioides* are seen in the background.

| LANTANA CAMARA | *Verbenaceae* | 26°F. |
|---|---|---|
| Bush lantana | All Year | American tropics |

The bush lantanas, particularly the dwarf forms, function well in many types of plantings. They can be treated as annual bedding plants in cold areas. Many named cultivars of this species and of hybrids with *Lantana montevidensis* offer a size range from one to six feet and flower colors in yellow, pink, white, orange and red.

Lantanas are tolerant of heat and drought but may occasionally be attacked by insects. They are notable for producing abundant flowers over a long season. These plants adapt so well that they have run wild in parts of the tropics, particularly Hawaii, where they are serious pests. For dependable color over long periods few other plants can match the many lantana varieties.

LIMONIUM PEREZII | *Plumbaginaceae* | 28°F.
Sea lavender, statice | Spring-Fall | Canary Islands

This attractive herbaceous perennial from the Canary Islands is so well-adapted to the climate of the coastal areas of southern California that it has become naturalized in many places on the rocky cliffs near the seashore. The long-lasting purplish-blue flower clusters are produced over a very long period. The plant does not stand much frost, but where temperatures permit, it deserves far wider use than it has had.

The photo shows sea lavender with *Chrysanthemum coronarium*, an annual, frequently naturalized along the coast where it forms large masses of color.

| PELARGONIUM PELTATUM | *Geraniaceae* | 27°F. |
| --- | --- | --- |
| Ivy geranium | Spring-Fall | South Africa |

Ivy geranium is used widely in California in mild coastal areas for spectacular effect. A species with trailing stems and somewhat fleshy succulent leaves, flower types and colors are numerous and appealing to collectors. White, pink, lavender and rose are colors most commonly seen. They require some attention including periodic replanting to keep them in good condition. On page 153 they are seen with bright yellow *Chrysanthemum coronarium*.

Illustrated above is *Pelargonium* X *domesticum* (Martha Washington geranium) which has a great variety of flower color and form with dark blotches on the two upper petals. Plants are erect to three feet or more and somewhat spreading. The showy flowers may be more than two inches across in loose clusters.

*Pelargonium* X *hortorum* shown above and on page 128 with *Plumbago auriculata* is the most common of the garden geraniums. It has varicolored leaves with flowers smaller but in fuller clusters than in Martha Washington types. It is used widely in California for outdoor massed color effects.

| PUYA SPATHACEA | *Bromeliaceae* | 27°F. |
| --- | --- | --- |
| | Early Summer | Argentina |

Shown in the picture above is one of the outdoor bromeliads grown in milder areas of the subtropics with spectacular effect. This relative of the pineapple has deep blue-green flowers but its rose-pink bracts and branching reddish flower stalks two to three feet high are more showy. It needs well-drained soil and must not be overwatered. *Puya alpestris* is taller with larger flowers having an unforgettable metallic blue-green color reminiscent of peacock feathers. *Puya chilensis* with chartreuse flowers is even more spectacular.

*Pelargonium peltatum*, see page 151

## SUCCULENTS FOR COLOR

The word "succulent" is a somewhat arbitrary term used for a very large number of plants which have in common thick fleshy leaves or stems making it possible for them to withstand an arid environment. All cacti are succulents but not all succulents are cacti. Because their water and care requirements are minimal while their landscaping effect can be maximal, they have become an important part of the landscape of southern California. Most prefer a mild climate but some can endure cold.

Most succulents are started easily by cuttings placed in the soil during periods of rainfall or irrigation. Highway plantings are started in this manner in areas near the coast. Sometimes the rosette types such as *Echeveria* are planted close together to produce a sheet of almost solid color from their foliage alone.

The succulents require little maintenance or pest control though dead stems and foliage should be cleared away. Succulents of appropriate types often are an ideal solution to landscape design when color at ground level is the objective. All plants described in pages 154 to 163 are succulents. They are propagated easily by cuttings rooted in sand.

| LAMPRANTHUS SPECTABILIS | *Aizoaceae* | 25°F. |
|---|---|---|
| Trailing ice plant | Spring | South Africa |

For a time, "ice plants" were almost too evident along California highways until *Carpobrotus edulis* with its rank growth, sparse but large flowers and tendency to slippage on steep slopes, gave way to better varieties. *Malephora purpureo-crocea* and *Delosperma* 'Alba' are now the most common of these South African natives because of their better growing habits and their inconspicuous flowers that do not distract motorists. In gardens other species are better for their splashes of brilliant color as illustrated on pages 131, 155, 156 and 160. *Drosanthemum speciosum* (page 155) is a small shrub with striking flowers of burnt orange with green centers. In contrast, *D. floribundum* forms thin purple-flowered sheets which hug the ground as illustrated on page 131 (low foreground) with *Pelargonium* X *domesticum* in the background. Among these also are an aloe, an agave and *Cordyline australis*, a tree from New Zealand having narrow stiff leaves giving a palm-like effect. Among the most showy of succulent ground covers are species of *Lampranthus*, such as *L. aurantiacus*, with large orange or yellow flowers, and *L. spectabilis* (pages 155 and 156), with purple flowers in great profusion. When out of bloom these species have great practical value as ground covers though with less character than when glowing with flowers. Most are best restarted every three or four years from cuttings which root easily in damp sand or even directly in the ground.

*Lampranthus* *Aloe striata* hybrid

AEONIUM CANARIENSE hybrid | *Crassulaceae* | 27°F.
Aeonium | Winter-Spring | Canary Islands

The many species of aeoniums are particularly showy near the ocean, thrive in milder inland areas, but will stand little frost. All are striking in form, consisting of rosettes of green or purple leaves frequently borne on branched stems up to several feet high. Aeoniums in the above photo show how well they have naturalized near the ocean in La Jolla. Their bright yellow cones are especially showy when mixed with aloes (*Aloe striata*), seen in the background of the picture. They are also shown on page 158 upper left behind *Kalanchoe*.

KALANCHOE BLOSSFELDIANA

*Crassulaceae* 28°F.
Winter-Spring Madagascar

The orange-red flowers in the foreground, left, are of *Kalanchoe blossfeldiana*, an excellent flowering pot-plant and useful for flaming winter and spring color outdoors. In mild areas it provides spectacular color for a long period of time and is particularly striking when contrasted to brilliant yellow-flowered aeoniums as shown here.

CRASSULA FALCATA

*Crassulaceae* 27°F.
Summer-Fall South Africa

The showy red flowers of this succulent plant have made it a favorite of plant collectors. The attractive flowers keep well when cut and are prized by floral decorators. The unusual gray-bluish sickle-shaped leaves are closely clustered at the base of the stem and provide an interesting contrast with pebbles or colored mulch materials. As with other succulents, watering may be casual.

SEDUM DENDROIDEUM PRAEALTUM *Crassulaceae* 25°F.

Spring-Summer Mexico

Both the species and the variants of this succulent are useful for massed plantings. They have attractive foliage, borne on stems several feet high. This variety illustrated in the background in the photograph above has green leaves and clear yellow flowers. Little water or care is required. The plants grow readily from cuttings set in the ground and thrive best in sunny locations, in well-drained soil. This species is tender, but other hardier species available make very refined, satisfactory ground covers. They are useful for planting on dry walls.

The photograph also shows *Sedum cupressoides*, in the right foreground, a decumbent, evergreen perennial with cypress-like leaves and bright yellow flowers, blooming in July and August. Across the path the yucca-like plant with the red flowering stems is *Beschorneria yuccoides* surrounded at the base by gray-leaved *Crassula deltoides*. *Sedum* X *rubrotinctum* is in the left foreground and is more conspicuous in the retaining wall structure shown on page 160. This is a smaller species noted for the plump rounded leaves which often become ruddy-colored in the sun. Plants may be grown from leaves or stem cuttings. The flowers are yellow. The upright plants growing with the *Sedum* are *Kalanchoe tubiflora* from Madagascar.

*Sedum X rubrotinctum*

AGAVE
Century plants

*Agavaceae* 29°F.
Various North and South America

Forbidding as their spiky leaves may appear, agaves add a dramatic touch to the subtropical garden. Their bold rosettes are beautifully symmetrical and seem appropriate to the hot and arid southwest; see page 131 and in the right foreground on page 151.

Commonest is *A. americana,* with gigantic clusters of bluish-gray leaves useful in a background planting. Several of its variegated cultivars, such as on page 131, are even more decorative. Beloved of professional landscapers is *A. attenuata,* the fox-tail agave, so named for its arching-pendent brush of flowers; its leaves are pliable and spineless but easily damaged by frosts. Related and most desirable is *A. vilmoriniana,* with an erect twenty foot column of golden yellow flowers. It does not have offset rosettes but dies after flowering producing hundreds of young plants on the inflorescence. *A. filifera,* an excellent rockery plant, has foot-wide clusters of white-streaked, thread-margined leaves and bottle-brush-like flower stalks.

Also small but with wide handsome gray leaves are *A. huachucensis* and *A. shawii,* the latter illustrated on this page along with blue lance leaves of a *Yucca.* Shaw's agave, a California native plant, is found in a few areas just north of the Mexican border. This agave's nine foot stem arises from the typical fleshy-leaved rosette screened in the illustration by yucca leaves and bears greenish-yellow flowers in open heads sometime between September and May. This species is most at home in a desert type garden and demands little except well-drained soil.

Despite their common name, most century plants bloom every seven to fifteen years, those species not producing offsets perishing after flowering. Spiny types are best kept away from paths. Over 100 species can be seen at the Huntington Botanical Gardens.

ALOE | *Liliaceae* 22°F.
Winter, Spring, Summer South Africa

The aloes (pictured above, opposite and on pages 148, 156 and 157) are succulents which come mostly from various parts of Africa. They exist in a wide range of sizes and colors and provide colorful massed effects useful as ground cover plantings for some sites, as accent plants in others. Most bloom during winter months, but by combining species, the blooming season can be extended. Their inflorescences resemble red hot pokers with combinations and different shades of red, yellow and orange.

Aloes require infrequent watering. The old foliage should be cleared out as needed to maintain a neat appearance. Aloes root easily from stem cuttings planted directly in the ground. A notable collection of these plants is in the Huntington Botanical Gardens where the picture opposite was taken. A hybrid aloe is blooming in the foreground; the tall plant on the left is *Aloe africana* and the plant without flowers on the right is *A. dichotoma*. Additional aloes of merit are *A. bainesii*, a tender but impressive tree to 40 feet; *A. ferox*, slowly reaching 10 feet and with candelabras of orange flowers; and the shrubby *A. pluridens* and *A. arborescens*, both with highly colored floral displays. Smaller and for pots and borders are *A. variegata*, *A.X virens* and *A. brevifolia*.

*Aloe ciliaris* above, the climbing aloe, is not a true vine but a scrambling shrub, best

*Aloe africana* *A. dichotoma*

trained on walls or steep banks to display its orange-red green-tipped flowers of gem-like brilliance and distinction. A bit slow to start, the plant is probably best with a little shade, especially at its roots. It ultimately achieves eight feet or more with periodic bursts of flowers in stalked sprays some eight inches high. Although indifferent to soil, it will not tolerate continued freezing. Prune while flowering or immediately after.

# ANNUALS and PERENNIALS

Opposite is a chart showing some of the annuals and perennials useful as ground covers. Above are petunia hybrids usually grown as summer annuals in colder areas. Few plants equal petunias for eye-catching color in beds, borders, and window boxes. They are constantly being improved by plant breeders and are available in many different sizes, colors, and growth habits.

## ANNUALS AND PERENNIALS USEFUL FOR GROUND COVERS

| Species | Family | Common Name | Origin | Height to | Color | Season of Color |
|---|---|---|---|---|---|---|
| Bellis perennis | Compositae | English daisy | Europe | 6″ | several colors | winter-spring |
| Canna cultivars | Cannaceae | canna | Tropics | 6′ | various colors | summer |
| Chrysanthemum parthenium aureum | Compositae | golden feather | Eurasia | 3′ | white | summer |
| Coreopsis pubescens | Compositae | dwarf coreopsis | E. United States | 4′ | yellow | summer |
| Dianthus deltoides | Caryophyllaceae | maiden pink | Eurasia | 12″ | pink | spring, summer |
| D. plumarius | | cottage pink | Eurasia | 18″ | various colors | summer-fall |
| Iberis sempervirens | Cruciferae | evergreen candytuft | Eurasia | 18″ | white | winter-spring |
| Lobelia erinus | Lobeliaceae | annual lobelia | So. Africa | 6″ | blue | summer-fall |
| Lobularia maritima | Cruciferae | sweet alyssum | Europe | 6″ | several colors | year long |
| Malcolmia maritima | Cruciferae | Virginia stock | Europe | 15″ | several colors | winter-spring |
| Phlox drummondii | Polemoniaceae | dwarf annual phlox | Texas | 18″ | several colors | summer |
| Portulaca grandiflora | Portulacaceae | portulaca | Brazil | 6″ | many colors | summer |
| Salvia splendens | Labiatae | scarlet sage | Brazil | 3′ | scarlet | summer |
| Sanvitalia procumbens | Compositae | | Mexico | 6″ | yellow and purple | summer |
| Tagetes patula | Compositae | French marigold | Mexico | 18″ | yellow-brown | summer |
| Thymophylla tenuiloba | Compositae | Dahlberg daisy, golden fleece | Mexico | 12″ | yellow | summer-fall |
| Verbena hybrida | Verbenaceae | garden verbena | garden | 12″ | various colors | summer |
| Viola cornuta | Violaceae | viola | So. Europe | 8″ | various colors | winter-spring |
| V. odorata | | sweet violet | Eurasia-Africa | 6″ | various colors | spring |
| V. tricolor hortensis | | pansy | garden | 8″ | various colors | winter-spring |
| Zinnia, dwarf types | Compositae | zinnia | Mexico | 12″ | many colors | summer |

## ADDITIONAL PLANTS FOR COLOR ON THE GROUND

| Species | Family | Common Name | Origin | Height to | Color | Season of Color | Hardy to |
|---|---|---|---|---|---|---|---|
| Achillea tomentosa | Compositae | woolly yarrow | Eurasia | 10″ | yellow | summer | 0°F. |
| Armeria maritima | Plumbaginaceae | sea pink | Europe | 12″ | pink | most of year | 0°F. |
| Begonia semperflorens | Begoniaceae | bedding begonias | Brazil | 18″ | white to rose | summer-fall | 35°F. |
| Bergenia crassifolia | Saxifragaceae | winter-blooming bergenia | Himalayas | 20″ | rose or lilac | winter | 15°F. |
| Campanula elatines garganica | Campanulaceae | bellflower | So. Europe | 6″ | violet | summer | 0°F. |
| C. poscharskyana | | Serbian bellflower | Europe | 12″ | blue | spring-summer | 0°F. |
| Carissa macrocarpa, dwarf cultivars—See p. 63. | | | | | | | |
| Centaurea cineraria | Compositae | dusty miller | Europe | 12″ | purple | summer | 20°F. |
| Ceratostigma griffithii | Plumbaginaceae | Burmese plumbago | India | 2′-3′ | blue | summer | 27°F. |
| C. plumbaginoides | | dwarf plumbago | China | 12″ | bluish | summer | 15°F. |
| C. willmottianum | | Chinese plumbago | China | 4′ | blue | summer-fall | 15°F. |
| Cistus hybrids | Cistaceae | rockrose | Mediterranean | 5′ | various colors | summer | 20°F. |
| Cotoneaster, several low shrubby species | Rosaceae | cotoneaster | Asia | 3′ | white flowers, red fruit | summer-winter | 15°F. |
| Erigeron karvinskianus | Compositae | vittadinia | Mexico-Panama | 20″ | white | summer-fall | 15°F. |
| Helianthemum nummularium | Cistaceae | sunrose | Mediterranean | 8″ | various | spring, summer | 20°F. |
| Hemerocallis cultivars | Liliaceae | daylily | Asia | 6′ | yellow to bronze-red | most of year | 10°F. |
| Iris cultivars | Iridaceae | iris | world-wide | 4′ | many colors | most of year | 0°F. |

| | Family | Common Name | Origin | Height to | Color | Season of Color | Hardy to |
|---|---|---|---|---|---|---|---|
| Lotus berthelotii | Leguminosae | parrot's beak | Canary Islands | 2′ | scarlet | summer | 27°F. |
| L. corniculatus | | birdsfoot trefoil | Eurasia | 6″ | yellowish | summer-fall | 10°F. |
| L. mascaensis | | | Canary Islands | 2′ | yellow | summer | 25°F. |
| Lysimachia nummularia | Primulaceae | moneywort | Europe | 3″ | yellow | summer | 0°F. |
| Mazus reptans | Scrophulariaceae | | Himalayas | 2″ | blue | spring-summer | 0°F. |
| Myoporum parvifolium | Myoporaceae | | Australia | 3″ | white | summer | 25°F. |
| Oenothera speciosa | Onagraceae | Mexican evening primrose | Mexico, Texas | 12″ | pink | summer | 20°F. |
| Oxypetalum caeruleum | Asclepiadaceae | | Argentina | 2′ | blue | summer | 27°F. |
| Phyla nodiflora *(Lippia repens)* | Verbenaceae | lippia | Tropics | 3″ | lilac-rose | spring-fall | 20°F. |
| Plumbago auriculata *(P. capensis)* | Plumbaginaceae | cape plumbago | So. Africa | 10′ | white-blue | most of year | 25°F. |
| Ranunculus repens | Ranunculaceae | creeping buttercup | No. Temperate | 2′ | yellow | spring | Hardy |
| Rosa—some climbing sorts make good bank covers, see p. 103 | | | | | | | |
| Rosmarinus officinalis 'Prostratus' | Labiatae | creeping rosemary | Mediterranean | 2′ | blue | winter-spring | 10°F. |
| Santolina chamaecyparissus | Compositae | lavender cotton | Mediterranean | 2′ | yellow | summer | 20°F. |
| S. virens | | green santolina | Europe | 2′ | chartreuse | summer | 20°F. |
| Saxifraga stolonifera *(S. sarmentosa)* | Saxifragaceae | strawberry geranium | E. Asia | 2′ | light pink | spring | Tender |
| Teucrium chamaedrys 'Prostratum' | Labiatae | prostrate germander | Europe | 6″ | lavender | summer | Hardy |
| Trachelospermum jasminoides | Apocynaceae | star jasmine | So. China | 2′ | white | summer | 20°F. |
| Verbena peruviana cultivars | Verbenaceae | | So. America | 18″ | various colors | summer | 27°F. |
| V. tenera | | sand verbenas | Brazil | 18″ | various colors | summer | 20°F. |
| Vinca major | Apocynaceae | periwinkle | Europe | 12″ | lilac-blue | various | 0°F. |
| V. minor | | periwinkle | Europe | 12″ | blue and lilac-blue | various | 0°F. |

THEODORE PAYNE
*Fremontodendron* hybrid

Largely due to the efforts of one man, California wild flowers are found in gardens all over the world. This man was Theodore Payne in whose honor a California native plant foundation was established in 1960. The Theodore Payne Foundation operates a nursery, art gallery and library on 22 acres at 10459 Tuxford Street, Sun Valley, California.

When Theodore Payne was a young lad hunting wild flowers in the hills around Northampshire, England, an event occurred at the Royal Botanic Gardens at Kew that was to shape his entire life. An exhibit of plants collected by Archibald Menzies in far-off California drew large crowds and captured the hearts of avid English gardeners. When he was 21 Payne headed for California where he found the people largely unaware of the bountiful floral array nature had bestowed. He immediately set about collecting seeds and heralding the native flora.

Theodore Payne brought some 430 native species into cultivation and through his efforts seed was sent throughout the world. Many native plantings, including Exposition Park in Los Angeles, were done by Payne. He was much interested in Ralph Cornell's development of Torrey Pines Park and the campus of Pomona College. Payne selected the original site of Rancho Santa Ana Botanic Garden and inspired the establishment of the Santa Barbara Botanic Garden. Many honors came to Theodore Payne before his death in 1963. The world has benefitted from his contributions to gardens.

## TIPS FOR GROWING CALIFORNIA NATIVE PLANTS

Since the times of the earliest explorers, California has been famous for the beauty of its native plants. But it was Theodore Payne who found some of nature's secrets for successful seed germination and culture. His discovery that matilija poppy seeds need the scorching heat of brush fires to germinate, initiated a technique now used for many recalcitrant seeds.

Through years of observation and experimentation he found most native plants should be set out in the fall because winter rains are crucial. No fertilizer or soil amendments should be used in planting. During the first year, watering every two weeks is usually required. Except for plants whose native habitat is moist or damp, they need sharp drainage especially at the soil surface and little or no watering after plants have become established.

California's annual wildflowers are sown in the fall. Those of perennial wildflowers can be started in the spring in seed flats and will often bloom the following year. Some germinate readily while others need special treatment such as a combination of moisture and low temperature. Such seeds may be mixed with fine moist sand or peat moss and refrigerated for several weeks to break dormancy.

Californians are especially fortunate that a wide array of flowering plants are well-adapted to the state's semi-arid climate. Through the years plants from all over the world have been introduced, but meanwhile the native plants have survived in the very environment to which imports must become adapted. Many California natives can be grown away from their natural range but if temperatures or evaporation rates differ greatly from those of their native habitat, their culture should be considered experimental.

Additional California native plants of merit are listed on page 203.

## ESCHSCHOLZIA CALIFORNICA
California poppy

*Papaveraceae* Ground cover
Spring Annual

When California's spring pageant of wild flowers was first noted by Spanish explorers from the ships off the coast, the California poppy, now the state flower, grew in unbelievable quantities. Its display, much diminished now, still enlivens many areas. The poppy is easily grown from seed. It should be raked in lightly in the fall, then kept moist until the rains begin. Seed sown in mid-spring will produce summer flowers of somewhat smaller size. It is usually grown as an annual but often re-seeds. Though it tolerates a wide variety of soils, it does best in the lighter ones.

The many species of the California poppy vary from large flowers with deep orange hues to small yellow cups with orange tipped petals. Charming garden selections run the gamut of color from white to red and even pink, single and double.

Among the poppies in the landscape above (taken at Santa Barbara Botanic Garden) are baby blue eyes or *Nemophila menziesii*, tidy tips or *Layia platyglossa* ssp. *campestris*, and the brilliant yellow sea dahlia, *Coreopsis maritima*, a close relative of the giant coreopsis shown on page 181.

*Eschscholzia californica* *Nemophila menziesii* *Layia platyglossa* *Coreopsis maritima*
Famous California native plant exhibits may be seen at:
Native Plant Garden, Descanso Gardens, 1418 Descanso Dr., La Cañada,
Rancho Santa Ana Botanic Garden, 1500 N. College Ave., Claremont,
Santa Barbara Botanic Garden, 1212 Mission Canyon Rd., Santa Barbara, California
Theodore Payne Foundation, 10459 Tuxford Street, Sun Valley, California

ARCTOSTAPHYLOS INSULARIS — *Ericaceae* — Shrub

Island manzanita — Winter — Evergreen

Manzanitas are an important part of hilly California landscapes. Their bright reddish bark on distinctly crooked stems, with green or gray-green ovate leaves which maintain their healthy appearance the year around, sets them apart even at a distance. When established,manzanitas are drought resistant and need little or no water during summer months.

Island manzanita, native to Santa Cruz and Santa Rosa Islands, is an erect six foot, much-branched shrub, particularly attractive for its smooth shiny elliptical one to two inch leaves and red-brown stems. In mid-winter or early spring spreading panicles of small waxy white flowers appear followed by yellow-brown fruit called "little apples" by early settlers. This plant is valuable on dry slopes for its year-long color. Propagation by seed is slow and difficult but cuttings can be rooted rather easily.

The pink-bracted manzanita, *Arctostaphylos pringlei* var. *drupacea,* native to southern California mountains, is upright growing to 12 feet. Except for the smooth red-brown branches all other parts of the shrub are covered with fine hairs. Delightful fragrant rose-pink flower clusters with pink bracts cover the plant in spring.

*Arctostaphylos edmundsii,* the Little Sur manzanita, is an attractive low shrub or ground cover for full shade or full sun. Pink flowers are showy in mid-winter.

Many other species and named cultivars are available.

*Arctostaphylos pringlei* var. *drupacea*

*Arctostaphylos insularis*

BERBERIS (MAHONIA) NEVINII | *Berberidaceae* | Shrub
Nevin's barberry | Spring | Evergreen

Nevin's barberry, now almost extinct in the wild, has become well established in southern California gardens. It is valuable for its distinctly bluish foliage and yellow flowers in short racemes followed in late summer by reddish berries. It forms a dense shrub to 10 feet tall with arching branches reaching to the ground. The growth habit and its prickly leaves make it useful both as a hedge as well as for shelter and food for birds when considering plants for a sanctuary. This barberry is especially tolerant of drought, being native to hot sandy areas, but it is also amenable to ordinary garden culture. It may be grown from seed or from nursery stock. This particular form, native to the San Fernando Valley, was saved from extinction by Theodore Payne.

*Berberis (Mahonia) pinnata*, the California mahonia, is a four foot shrub for moist, partly shaded locations. Its fragrant yellow blooms are succeeded by glaucous blue berries.

*Berberis (Mahonia) repens*, creeping mahonia, is a good ground cover for partial shade. See page 75 for other mahonias.

*Berberis aquifolium*

## CERCIS OCCIDENTALIS
Western redbud

*Leguminosae* Tree-shrub
Spring Deciduous

Redbud in bloom commands attention in early spring with its mass of red-purple flowers on bare branches making this one of the most showy native trees or large shrubs. Occasionally a white-flowered form is seen. The somewhat divided, heart-shaped leaves are of interest after the flowers are gone. Brown pendent pods appear in fall. Accustomed to dry summers and cold winters, it is a hardy plant and admirably fills the need for a small deciduous tree in thin inland soils. Redbud starts easily from seeds but growth is slow. *C. canadensis* (eastern United States) and *C. siliquastrum* (Europe) are 30 foot trees with rosy-pink flowers.

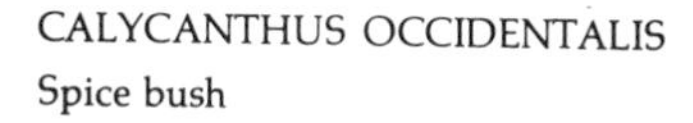

## CALYCANTHUS OCCIDENTALIS
Spice bush

*Calycanthaceae* Shrub
Spring-Summer Deciduous

*Calycanthus occidentalis,* known as both spice bush or sweet shrub, is a large spreading shrub to nine feet. The ovate two to six inch leaves are harsh to the touch but fragrant when crushed. Their rich dark green color makes for a cool lush appearance. Flowers, borne singly at branch ends, are nestled among the foliage. The large, deep red, many petaled blossoms, unique in California native species, appear from spring through midsummer.

Sweet shrub, found throughout the northern coast ranges and Sierra Nevada foothills in cool moist canyons, can be used where a background plant is needed in a shaded spot having year-round moisture.

CHILOPSIS LINEARIS
Desert willow

| *Bignoniaceae* | Shrub-tree |
| --- | --- |
| Spring-Summer | Deciduous |

Desert willow is a large spreading shrub or small tree found in desert washes. In late spring and summer large, fragrant, catalpa-like flowers in white to pink or lavender with darker lines grace slender arching branches. The blossoms are followed by thin narrow pods containing many flat seeds with a tuft of hairs at each end. The narrow, willow-like leaves are shed in winter to reveal a framework of limbs with shredded bark. Desert willow should be watered moderately or else grown where loose soil allows the roots to penetrate to a supply of moisture below. It does best inland. Near the coast it should be placed in as warm a location as possible.

FALLUGIA PARADOXA
Apache plume

| *Rosaceae* | Shrub |
| --- | --- |
| Spring | Deciduous |

Apache plume, native of the pinyon-juniper woodland of the eastern Mojave Desert, is a low shrub to five feet. In late spring one to one and a half inch white flowers are produced singly at the ends of the branches, followed by small dry fruits with persistent feathery, plume-like styles which give the plant its picturesque name. The many branchlets are covered with a noticeable thin flaky bark. The small leaves are divided into a number of narrow leaflets with incurved edges.

Apache plume, because of its native habitat, is tolerant of temperature extremes and considerable drought and wind.

| CHRYSOTHAMNUS | *Compositae* | Shrub |
|---|---|---|
| Rabbit brush | Fall | Deciduous |

Chrysothamnus, usually known as rabbit brush, gives to the high desert much of its fall color, when these bushy plants with their panicles of showy yellow flowers often dominate the landscape. The small, narrow, gray-green leaves are at this time less noticeable compared to the heady show of bloom. The shrub may be from two to as much as ten feet tall. It is quite tolerant of alkali and grows on plains and slopes alike.

Rabbit brush can be used where late season bloom is desired and the fine grayish foliage is acceptable, especially where hot summers and severe winters limit the selection of plant materials.

This can be a valuable plant for erosion control on steep loose banks where summers are warm and dry. These shrubs are frequently used on road fills.

Penstemon cordifoliu

| PENSTEMON CORDIFOLIUS<br>*(Keckiella)* | *Scrophulariaceae* | Perennial |
| --- | --- | --- |
| Heart-leaved penstemon | Spring-Summer | Semi-deciduous |

Of the nearly 60 penstemons found in California, many of which are handsome garden subjects, this species is one of the few that is half-climbing in habit and therefore is sometimes known as "climbing penstemon." The leaves are somewhat heart-shaped, smooth and dark green with strong veining, and up to two inches long. The dull scarlet flowers appear in late spring and early summer in compact drooping panicles borne upside down. This plant is often seen draping down roadside banks where a single plant may cover several square yards. Near the coast it prefers a sunny slope but inland it keeps better foliage if shaded for a part of the day. It can be propagated from seed or cuttings.

Many species of penstemon are desirable ornamentals. Among the native species recommended are *P. grinnellii*, a spring and summer bloomer with pinkish-white flowers; *P. heterophyllus* with rose-violet flowers in spring and summer; and *P. palmeri* with pinkish-white flowers in spring. These three species are perennial herbs, the first two reaching about one and a half feet in height and the latter four feet.

Zauschneria cana

ZAUSCHNERIA CANA | *Onagraceae* | Herbaceous perennial
California fuchsia | Summer-Fall | Evergreen

This member of the evening primrose family has long been cultivated for its showy red blossoms which continue from late summer throughout the fall. The flowers are long funnel-form, flaring at the ends and an inch or so long. California fuchsia is found from Monterey to Los Angeles counties and on the Channel Islands.

The plant, as well as the more common Z. *californica*, is particularly useful on slopes or in the rock garden as a ground cover where it forms a fairly dense mat 18 inches or more across and perhaps two feet high. In the shade it often grows erect. When planted rather closely and pinched back it fills in nicely to produce color at a time when flowers are scarce.

PICKERINGIA MONTANA | *Leguminosae* | Shrub
Chaparral pea (above) | Spring-Summer | Evergreen

Large reddish-purple pea-shaped flowers in the spring and summer set this shrub apart from the many small-leaved shrubs of the chaparral community. This evergreen plant, three to six feet in height, has stiff spiny branches and olive-green leaves of less than a half inch in length. Flat one to two-inch pods are produced only rarely and the plant depends more for propagation on rooting underground stems. It is at home in California on dry slopes of the coast ranges, especially from Santa Barbara County northward.

Under cultivation this shrub is primarily for dry hillside gardens. At the Santa Barbara Botanic Garden it has been rather difficult to establish in clay soil.

DENDROMECON RIGIDA | *Papaveraceae* | Shrub
Yellow tree poppy | Spring | Deciduous

Tree or bush poppy, the only native shrub member of the poppy family, makes a charming addition to drier gardens. Its large, clear yellow flowers are produced over a long season if water is given to supplement rainfall. In fact, some blossoms may be found at any time of the year. This is an open, stiffly branched plant usually between six and ten feet high. The narrow, leathery leaves are up to four inches long.

The island counterparts of the mainland species are *Dendromecon harfordii* and its variety *rhamnoides*, with slightly larger flowers and broader leaves. The habit of these plants is somewhat less stiff and there is a greater tendency to produce some flowers throughout the year.

Propagation by seed requires sowing in flats then burning over using straw or pine needles, followed by watering. Cuttings may be taken when plants are in full bloom or in summer from ripened wood.

| COREOPSIS GIGANTEA | *Compositae* | Woody perennial |
| --- | --- | --- |
| Giant coreopsis | Spring | Deciduous |

The giant coreopsis is unique among eleven California native species of this genus. A soft woody trunk up to four inches thick and from three to ten feet tall is crowned by several spreading branches. During most of the year the plant is leafless and will remain dormant even with summer watering. Growth resumes at the start of the rainy season when the branches soon become covered with finely dissected light green leaves up to a foot in length. The large three inch flowers follow early in the spring, their rich golden yellow adorning the coastal headlands in a striking manner.

| FREMONTODENDRON CALIFORNICUM | *Sterculiaceae* | Shrub |
|---|---|---|
| Flannel bush, fremontia | Spring | Evergreen |

Fremontia, known also as flannel bush and California slippery elm, is one of the most popular native shrubs. It is a large spreading plant 12 feet or more in height, and produces in late spring masses of two inch flowers of a strong clear yellow. The rounded, lobed leaves are dull green with tawny hairs beneath. It is tolerant of both heat and cold but is very sensitive to excess moisture. Good drainage and sparse summer watering are required.

*Fremontodendron mexicanum*, a species native to San Diego County and Baja California, has flowers to three and a half inches across. This plant is less showy because the blossoms are partly hidden among the leaves, though it blooms all spring.

Hybrids between the two species have been developed. 'California Glory' is a notable one which has a magnificent spring display with a longer blooming period than the parents with often a second lighter show of blossoms in early summer.

Ceanothus leucodermis

Ceanothus impressus

| CEANOTHUS LEUCODERMIS | *Rhamnaceae* | Shrub |
|---|---|---|
| Chaparral whitehorn | Spring | Semi-deciduous to evergreen |

This large spreading shrub has deep persistent roots which make it valuable in erosion control on dry, stony slopes where other plants would not survive. The stiff and spiny branchlets with small dull green leaves are covered in early spring with clusters of white to pale blue blossoms.

*C. impressus*, the Santa Barbara ceanothus, becomes a spreading plant with close-set branches to about five feet in height. In spring the small deep blue flowers are a pleasing foil against the dark green deeply grooved foliage. Though native on the coast it withstands the heat of interior valleys. Light sandy soil is preferred but, like all ceanothus, it should be watered sparingly. One of the most popular *Ceanothus* is the evergreen 'Julia Phelps.' It is a compact shrub and eventually forms a mound up to six feet high and ten feet across with pleasing dark blue flowers.

LEPTODACTYLON CALIFORNICUM
Prickly phlox

*Polemoniaceae* Shrub
Spring Evergreen

Anyone driving through California coast range canyons during spring may see a small shrub hanging from gravelly banks and bearing dense flower heads of deep rose pink. This is the prickly phlox. It not only cliff-hangs but may also be found on hot, well-drained slopes. A one to three foot shrub, it is sometimes straggly, sometimes compact. The clusters of short needle-like leaves are closely set. When out of bloom the shrub is inconspicuous, but the spring display of rich pink is an enjoyable sight.

MIMULUS (DIPLACUS) hybrids
Bush monkey flower

*Scrophulariaceae* Shrub
Spring-Summer Semi-deciduous

The shrubby species of *Mimulus* are often put in a separate genus *Diplacus* and are among the brightest and longest blooming of all the hillside plants. The red, yellow, orange and buff blossoms persist from early spring through late summer. Tubular flowers terminate in flaring notched or fluted lobes. The shrub is from one to four feet high and has small intricately branched stems with narrow, toothed, blutinous leaves to three inches long. Hybrids in selected colors are now available. The plants will bloom for months if watered from spring through late summer, then allowed to go dry in the fall.

*Mimulus (Diplacus)* hybrids

*Heteromeles arbutifolia*

| HETEROMELES (PHOTINIA) ARBUTIFOLIA | *Rosaceae* | Tree-shrub |
| --- | --- | --- |
| Christmas berry | Summer | Evergreen |

The California holly, toyon, or Christmas berry, is perhaps the most widely known of California native shrubs. From late fall to early spring its large clusters of bright red berries are seen on many hillsides. It has been protected by law for many years. The toyon grows to 10 feet high and 15 feet across. With proper pruning it can be developed into a tree. The dark green leathery leaves are narrowly oblong, finely toothed, and about four inches long. In early summer large dense clusters of small creamy white blossoms appear. The year 'round beauty of this evergreen has earned it a favored spot on lists of natives for general landscape use. In shady spots it becomes tall and leggy and in heavy soils is subject to root rot. Otherwise it is tolerant of summer watering. Native to the Channel Islands is a larger-berried form, the more desirable type for gardens.

*Carpenteria californica*

| CARPENTERIA CALIFORNICA | *Saxifragaceae* | Shrub |
|---|---|---|
| Tree-anemone | Spring-Summer | Evergreen |

Lovely is the word for *Carpenteria* in bloom. The white anemone-like flowers with inch long petals are borne in small clusters at the tips of erect branches. Flowers in late spring and early summer are succeeded by conical capsules with numerous fine seeds. The rather narrow opposite leaves, three inches or more in length, are dark green above but covered with a fine whitish hair on the under surface.

Tree-anemone is found naturally only in Fresno County at lower-middle elevations between the San Joaquin and Kings rivers. It is now frequently seen in cultivation and is at its best in part shade in sandy soil. With some summer watering it retains its good appearance through most of the season.

| ROMNEYA COULTERI | *Papaveraceae* | Perennial |
|---|---|---|
| Matilija poppy | Spring-Summer | Deciduous |

"Queen of California wild flowers" is the distinction accorded the matilija poppy, whose huge white blossoms make the plant a show piece from mid-spring through late summer. The size of the flowers is enhanced by the contrast between white crepe paper-like petals and rich yellow stamens.

Clustered stems rise from half woody bases to a height of three to seven feet. The large divided leaves are bluish green and run the full length of the stems. Plants may be started from seed though germination is somewhat difficult. They may also be propagated during the winter season from root cuttings or by separating parts of an old clump. The roots should not be disturbed more than is necessary, but, once established, the matilija poppy is extremely hardy. Plants should be allowed to go dry in late summer and the stems pruned in early winter to within a few inches of the ground.

| ENCELIA FARINOSA | *Compositae* | Shrub |
|---|---|---|
| Brittle bush, incienso | Spring | Evergreen |

In late March or April the gravelly mesas and washes of the desert come alive with the brilliant deep yellow blossoms of brittle bush. At this season the erect stems of the two to three foot mound-shaped shrubs are literally covered by daisy-like blooms which continue throughout the spring. During the remainder of the year the plant returns to its modest role of melting into the desert landscape, its light gray leaves on brittle stems drawing little attention from the passerby.

Brittle bush is best suited to sandy soil in the interior valleys and deserts. Its seasonal color and continuous fragrance, which prompted the Spanish name "incienso," make it well worth including in the desert garden.

# CALIFORNIA GOLD

In the golden fields of wild flowers characteristic of California's springtime, the flower which adds the most widespread touches of gold next to the California poppy is goldfields or sunshine, *Lasthenia chrysostoma*. This is the low growing annual seen in the field. It is a true yellow and so may be distinguished at a distance from the poppy.

Owl's clover, *Orthocarpus purpurascens*, identified by its purplish pink flowers among the goldfields, provides a color not often found in such large masses. The colors of these two plants growing under and around the valley oaks make the picture typical of the California springtime landscape.

| LAVATERA ASSURGENTIFLORA | *Malvaceae* | Shrub |
|---|---|---|
| Tree mallow | Spring to Fall | Evergreen |

The tree mallow, also known as malva rosa and California windbreak, is native to the Channel Islands but has long since been introduced to the coastal mainland. It is a spreading evergreen shrub up to 15 feet high and at least as broad. The lobed leaves grow to eight inches across. The flowers are rose-colored with darker veinings and they appear continuously from early spring to late fall.

This plant, because of its rapid growth and resistance to buffeting sea winds, has been widely used as a windbreak. It withstands some heat and is considered half hardy but is short-lived.

| DALEA SPINOSA | *Leguminosae* | Tree |
|---|---|---|
| Smoke tree (See page 193) | Summer | Deciduous |

The smoke tree of the low desert has always had a special appeal to artists and others sensitive to the beauty of that area. When seen from a distance the tree's smoky gray branches blend into the landscape, making it appear to be a link between the plant world and the atmosphere. In early summer it puts forth its inch long spikes of rich blue-violet flowers which cover the entire plant.

As a tree this species may reach a height of 18 feet but it frequently grows as a large spreading shrub. A coarse soil and good drainage appear to be necessary since this plant is almost exclusively confined to sandy washes. It is recommended as a garden subject only for desert areas. The hard seed coats are said to be scoured by the tumbling sand and gravel during storms, after which the seeds germinate more readily.

| TRICHOSTEMA LANATUM | *Labiatae* | Shrub |
| --- | --- | --- |
| Woolly blue curls | Spring-Summer | Evergreen |

Woolly blue curls, sometimes known as romero, is one of the most striking members of the mint family. It is an erect shrub growing from three to five feet tall, with narrow leaves two to three inches long, green above and light woolly beneath. The flowers, grouped along the upper part of the stem, are covered with dense woolly blue to purple hairs. Inch-long stamens issue from the blue flowers in a prominent, almost comical manner. Woolly blue curls is native to the dry hillsides and sandy flats of coastal regions from Monterey south.

This aromatic plant is one of the popular California native shrubs in cultivation where it flowers over a long season. Its requirements are minimal except for the need of good drainage. However the roots are very sensitive to disturbance during transplanting.

## AESCULUS CALIFORNICA

Buckeye, horse-chestnut

| *Hippocastanaceae* | Tree |
| --- | --- |
| Summer | Deciduous |

In the month of June, travelers in the foothills cannot help noticing a small tree or large shrub with prominent spikes of white flowers. This is the California buckeye and the state's only member of the buckeye family. It is found from Shasta and Siskiyou counties to northern Los Angeles County below 4000 feet in the Sierra Nevada and coast ranges.

Typically it is a round-topped tree of 15 to 20 feet. The showy compound leaves consist of leaflets two to six inches in length. The irregularly shaped flowers are about half an inch in length, hundreds of them clothing the ample erect or rarely pendulous spikes.

The trees are early deciduous, starting in July to reveal the light gray trunk and branches. This plant can be used where summer drought resistant specimens are needed and the early fall of leaves is acceptable.

## LYONOTHAMNUS FLORIBUNDUS ASPLENIFOLIUS

Catalina ironwood

| *Rosaceae* | Tree |
| --- | --- |
| Spring | Evergreen |

*Lyonothamnus*, named for an early Los Angeles forester and horticulturist, is one of the trees endemic to the Channel Islands. It is a slender tree under 50 feet in height with thin reddish brown bark which shreds off in narrow strips. Compound fern-like leaves give a softened appearance unlike that of most plants growing in the same environment. Small white flowers, borne in dense clusters at the tips of the branches, are succeeded by small pods. This variety is most commonly grown because of its finely notched foliage. It should be given good drainage and watered moderately.

*)alea spinosa*, see page 190.

*Calochortus kennedyi*

## CALOCHORTUS KENNEDYI

| Desert mariposa | *Liliaceae* | Bulb |
|---|---|---|
| | Spring | Deciduous |

Mariposa lilies excite the admiration of all who see them. Many colors are represented in the group but none are quite so intense as the orange to vermilion shades of the desert mariposa. The plant bears one to several broad cup-shaped flowers on stems from five to twenty inches high with a few narrow grass-like leaves arising from the ground. A native of the high deserts, this species is highly questionable as a garden subject.

Other species such as *C. catalinae, C. luteus, C. venustus, C. weedii,* and *C. vestae,* ranging in color from yellow and pink to white, are much more suitable but should be given excellent drainage and protection from rodents, especially gophers. The bulbs must remain dry during the summer.

The most suitable mariposa lily for garden culture is *C. vestae*. It may be grown from seed sown in flats in the fall and left until the following season before transplanting. They are more easily grown from bulbs placed in a special bed with good drainage.

## FOUQUIERIA SPLENDENS

Ocotillo

| *Fouquieriaceae* | Shrub |
|---|---|
| Spring | Deciduous |

Ocotillo is one of the desert's oddities. Most of the year its cluster of spiny canes appears almost lifeless. Soon after sufficient rain, small leaves appear and in spring the stems become tipped with panicles of scarlet flowers, giving the plant the appearance of lighted tapers. Within a few weeks the leaves and blossoms fall and the plant returns to dormancy.

Although most at home in the warmer deserts, ocotillo can be grown almost anywhere in the southern California lowlands as long as good drainage is provided and too much moisture is avoided. Plants may be started by simply cutting off a portion of a cane, which is dried for a few weeks and then set a few inches into the ground. Like most other desert plants, ocotillo is protected by law and should not be removed from public land.

*Yucca brevifolia*

## THE YUCCAS

In the late spring the chaparral country assumes a character unknown to it during the rest of the year. It is then that the yuccas send forth fast-growing flower stalks that culminate in a myriad of waxy cream-white blooms. The candles of bloom held aloft to the sky attract a host of insects of which the most important is the *Pronuba* moth which fertilizes the flowers and insures the plant's survival. *Yucca whipplei,* shown opposite and described on the following page, has several subspecies, some of which form a number of leaf rosettes. The rosette which flowers dies at the end of its blooming period. Other types which form only one group of leaves die completely after blooming but the thousands of flat black seeds give promise of another generation.

*Yucca brevifolia,* Joshua tree, ancient monarch of California deserts shown above is a famous native. Little known is the fact that it belongs to the genus *Yucca*. Joshua trees form a unique woodland covering many square miles in the Mojave Desert. In spring their grotesque forms produce tight clusters of white flowers at the tips of the branches, while underneath is usually found a colorful carpet of desert annuals. They are at home only in the desert garden where they can dominate the scene and provide a setting for many smaller desert plants. They need the summer heat of the interior for vigorous growth.

*Yucca whipplei*

## NOLINA PARRYI

Beargrass

| | |
|---|---|
| *Agavaceae* | Shrub-like plant |
| Spring | Evergreen |

Nolina resembles yucca with its showy flower stalk and myriads of blossoms. The individual blooms, however, are smaller than those of yucca and the male and female flowers are on separate plants. The flowers tend to be a deeper cream color. Parry's nolina is found both on desert slopes and in drier parts of the chaparral areas of southern California.

A giant relative of Parry's nolina, subspecies *wolfii*, grows on slopes of inland desert mountains. The flower stalk may reach a height of 12 feet with the other parts of the plant also larger in proportion. It provides a magnificent accent in its natural setting and a striking addition to the desert garden. Additional water will increase its rate of growth.

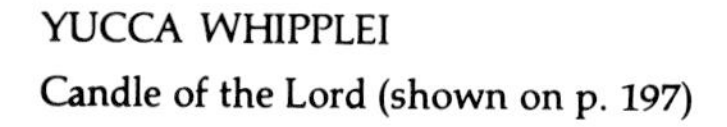

## YUCCA WHIPPLEI

Candle of the Lord (shown on p. 197)

| | |
|---|---|
| *Agavaceae* | Shrub-like plant |
| Spring-Summer | Evergreen |

Yucca in bloom is an accent plant of stunning beauty. In late spring or early summer a flower stalk bearing hundreds of pendent creamy white flowers grows with astonishing rapidity to a height of five to twelve feet out of the basal rosette of gray-green finely saw-toothed leaves. Later the blossoms mature into dry spongy capsules containing many flat black seeds.

Yucca is extremely persistent. After fires it sprouts new leaves, often from a charred and seemingly lifeless stump. This is a plant for the dry garden or an "impossible" slope but should be placed out of range of contact from its sharply pointed leaves. It may be grown from seed, with patience, or purchased from a nursery dealing with California natives.

*Cercidium floridum*

CERCIDIUM FLORIDUM
Palo verde

| *Leguminosae* | Tree |
| --- | --- |
| Spring-Summer | Deciduous |

Palo verde, Spanish for "green wood," is a tree of the desert washes in the Colorado desert. Most of the year the tree is bare. Its small compound leaves are produced only after rains. During dormant periods the function of the leaves is partly taken over by the blue-green stems and trunk. Sometime during the spring, as if to compensate, there is a notable display of small yellow blossoms on the spiny branchlets. Here again is an example of the predominance of yellow among California's native flowering plants. This tree withstands temperatures considerably below freezing for short periods.

# CACTI

Cacti account for some of the most distinctive native plants and are found throughout California. Many times they occur in company with yuccas, ocotillos and other xerophytes. Under cultivation cacti grow and thrive in most areas except where extremely cold or humid. The desert types will withstand some frost. Good drainage is essential and it is safest to plant them in beds raised well above the immediate surroundings. The bloom occurs irregularly from early to late spring.

The best source for cacti is a nursery dealing in these plants, but those willing to devote the necessary time can grow them from seed.

| ECHINOCEREUS ENGELMANNII | *Cactaceae* | Succulent |
|---|---|---|
| Hedgehog cactus | Spring | Evergreen |

The hedgehog cactus forms low clumps of erect cylinder-shaped branches arising from the ground. Each branch has a dozen or so ribs and is set with stout spines in a variety of colors: red, white, gray, yellow and brown. Its appearance has prompted the name cucumber cactus. The flowers are crimson-magenta. This plant is found in coarse soils on slopes and benches in many locations in the California deserts.

*Opuntia ficus-indica*

| OPUNTIA LITTORALIS | *Cactaceae* | Succulent |
|---|---|---|
| Prickly pear, tuna cactus | Spring | Evergreen |

Prickly pear is the name given to the many species of the genus *Opuntia* with flattened joints and juicy fruits which were relished by the Indians and are still sold in some markets of the southwest. *Opuntia littoralis* forms a many-branched shrub up to a yard or more in height. While most frequently it is used as an accent shrub in gardens, in many older gardens it was sometimes used as a fence. In time the prickly pear can provide a fire retardant barrier of considerable value. In late spring attractive yellow blossoms appear around the edge of its flattened joints. It is easily propagated from cuttings placed directly in sandy, well-drained soil, and it requires little water.

| FEROCACTUS ACANTHODES | *Cactaceae* | Succulent |
|---|---|---|
| Barrel cactus | Spring | Evergreen |

The well known barrel cactus was once a familiar sight on desert slopes. Now, though protected by law, it has been largely removed from the more accessible sites. When young it is globular in shape but in time assumes the typical barrel form. A ring of yellow flowers appears in spring at the crown of the plant. The size and form of this cactus with its spiny, fluted sides, are its salient features. Although it contains a great deal of moisture, the sap is unpalatable, a very poor substitute for a drink of clear water.

## ADDITIONAL COLORFUL CALIFORNIA NATIVE PLANTS OF MERIT

| Species | Family | Common Name | Habit | Height to | Color | Season of Color |
|---|---|---|---|---|---|---|
| Abronia villosa | Nyctaginaceae | desert verbena | herb | 1½′ | purplish-rose | winter-summer |
| Acacia greggii | Leguminosae | sweet acacia | shrub | 6′ | yellow | spring |
| Antirrhinum nuttallianum | Scrophulariaceae | violet snapdragon | herb | 3′ | violet | spring-summer |
| Aquilegia eximia | Ranunculaceae | Van Houtte's columbine | herb | 3′ | scarlet | spring-summer |
| Arabis blepharophylla | Cruciferae | coast rock cress | herb | 8″ | rose-purple | winter-spring |
| Arbutus menziesii | Ericaceae | madrone | tree | 70′ | white to pink | winter-spring |
| Armeria maritima californica | Plumbaginaceae | sea thrift | herb | 1½′ | pink | spring |
| Aster greatai | Compositae | Greata's aster | herb | 4′ | light purple | summer-fall |
| Beloperone californica | Acanthaceae | chuparosa | shrub | 5′ | scarlet-red | spring-summer |
| Bloomeria crocea | Amaryllidaceae | golden stars | herb | 2′ | orange-yellow | spring |
| Brodiaea elegans | Amaryllidaceae | harvest brodiaea | herb | 1½′ | purple | spring-summer |
| B. ida-maia | | firecracker flower | herb | 3′ | bright red | spring-summer |
| B. lutea | | golden brodiaea | herb | 2½′ | golden-yellow | spring-fall |
| Calliandra eriophylla | Leguminosae | fairy duster | shrub | 3′ | rose | winter-spring |
| Cassia armata | Leguminosae | senna | shrub | 3½′ | yellow | spring |
| Clarkia species | Onagraceae | clarkia, godetia | annual herb | 3½′ | white, pink to purple | spring-summer |
| Collinsia heterophylla | Scrophulariaceae | Chinese houses | annual herb | 1½′ | rose-purple | spring |
| Comarostaphylis diversifolia | Ericaceae | summer holly | shrub | 15′ | white | spring |
| Cornus nuttallii | Cornaceae | mountain dogwood | tree | 75′ | white | spring-summer |

| Species | Family | Common Name | Habit | Height to | Color | Season of Color |
|---|---|---|---|---|---|---|
| Crossosoma californicum | Crossosomataceae | crabapple bush | shrub | 6′ | white | winter-spring |
| Delphinium cardinale | Ranunculaceae | scarlet larkspur | herb | 6′ | scarlet | spring-summer |
| D. parryi | | Parry's larkspur | herb | 3′ | purplish-blue | spring |
| Dicentra formosa | Fumariaceae | bleeding heart | herb | 1½′ | rose-purple | spring-summer |
| Dudleya species | Crassulaceae | live-forever | succulent herb | 2½′ | white, yellow, red | spring-summer |
| Enceliopsis argophylla | Compositae | Panamint daisy | herb | 4′ | yellow | spring |
| Erigeron glaucus | Compositae | seaside daisy | herb | 1′ | violet-lavender | spring-summer |
| Eriogonum arborescens | Polygonaceae | island buckwheat | shrub | 5′ | white | summer |
| E. crocatum | | Conejo buckwheat | herb | 1′ | sulfur-yellow | spring-summer |
| E. giganteum | | St. Catherine's lace | shrub | 6′ | white | summer |
| Galvezia speciosa | Scrophulariaceae | island snapdragon | vining shrub | 3′ | red | spring |
| Gilia tricolor | Polemoniaceae | bird's eye gilia | annual herb | 1½′ | yellow, blue-violet | spring |
| Holodiscus discolor | Rosaceae | cream bush | shrub | 18′ | creamy-white | spring-summer |
| Hypericum formosum scouleri | Hypericaceae | St. John's wort | herb | 2½′ | yellow | summer |
| Iris, several species and hybrids | Iridaceae | iris | herb | 3′ | various colors | spring |
| Isomeris arborea | Capparaceae | bladder pod | shrub | 5′ | yellow | most of year |
| Lathyrus splendens | Leguminosae | Campo pea | vine | 10′ | crimson | spring |
| Lepechinia calycina | Labiatae | pitcher sage | shrub | 4′ | pinkish | spring |
| Lilium humboldtii | Liliaceae | Humboldt's lily | herb | 6′ | orange-yellow | summer |

| Species | Family | Common Name | Habit | Height to | Color | Season of Color |
|---|---|---|---|---|---|---|
| Lobelia cardinalis | Lobeliaceae | scarlet lobelia | herb | 3½′ | bright red | summer-fall |
| Lonicera involucrata | Caprifoliaceae | twinberry | shrub | 10′ | yellow | summer |
| Lupinus, several species | Leguminosae | lupine | herb-shrubs | 2″-6′ | various colors | spring-summer |
| Mentzelia lindleyi | Loasaceae | blazing star | annual herb | 2′ | golden-yellow | spring |
| Mimulus cardinalis | Scrophulariaceae | scarlet monkeyflower | herb | 2½′ | scarlet | spring-fall |
| Monolopia lanceolata | Compositae | hilltop daisy | annual herb | 2′ | bright yellow | spring |
| Phacelia campanularia | Hydrophyllaceae | bell-flowered phacelia | annual herb | 2′ | deep blue | spring |
| Philadelphus lewisii gordonianus | Saxifragaceae | Gordon's syringa | shrub | 10′ | white | spring-summer |
| Ribes aureum | Saxifragaceae | golden currant | shrub | 6′ | yellow | spring |
| R. malvaceum | | pink flowering currant | shrub | 6′ | rose | winter-spring |
| R. sanguineum | | fuchsia-flowered gooseberry | shrub | 9′ | red | spring |
| Rosa nutkana | Rosaceae | Nootka rose | shrub | 6′ | rose-pink | spring-summer |
| Salvia clevelandii | Labiatae | blue sage | shrub | 3′ | blue-purple | spring-summer |
| S. spathacea | | crimson sage | herb | 3′ | purplish-red | spring |
| Sisyrinchium bellum | Iridaceae | blue-eyed grass | herb | 1½′ | violet to blue | spring |
| Sphaeralcea ambigua | Malvaceae | desert mallow | herb or shrub | 3½′ | apricot | spring |
| Stanleya pinnata | Cruciferae | golden prince's plume | herb | 5′ | yellow | spring-summer |
| Styrax officinalis | Styracaceae | snowdrop bush | shrub | 12′ | white | spring |

# INDEX



*Illustrated

*Illustrated

*Illustrated

*Illustrated

*Illustrated